SEPHARDIM
The Spirit that has Withstood The Times

SEPHARDIM
The Spirit that has Withstood The Times

Piet Huisman

Huisman Editions, The Netherlands

Sephardim,
The Spirit that has Withstood The Times.
Includes index.
Jewish History-illustrated.
ISBN 90-9001386-5

Published by *Huisman Editions*,
P.O. Box 145,
5690 AC Son,
The Netherlands.

CIP-GEGEVENS
KONINKLIJKE BIBLIOTHEEK, DEN HAAG
Huisman, Piet

Sephardim : the spirit that has withstood the times /
Piet Huisman ; [ed. Bart de Vries ; transl. from the Dutch]. –
Son en Breughel : Huisman. – Ill.
Vert. van: Sefardiem : de stenen spreken/speaking stones.
– Son : Huisman, 1984. – Met index, lit. opg.
ISBN 90-9001386-5 geb.
SISO az.w-isra 944.7 UDC 933.4/.5
Trefw.: Sefardiem ; geschiedenis.

All proceeds of this book will go to the Library
Ets Haim, Amsterdam, The Netherlands.

Dedicated to Mary, my wife, my children and
grandchildren, the Sephardi communities in
the Netherlands and in the Dutch Antilles.

Contents

Introductions

The history of the Western Sephardim is a fascinating and colourful story. The term Western is nowadays used to distinguish between two groups. First the Spanish Jews that after the Expulsion from Spain in 1492 first fled to Portugal and from there moved on to establish themselves permanently in some of the Western European nations. Secondly the Jews that sought refuge in North Africa and the countries of the Mediterranean. It is with this first group of Sephardim that Piet Huisman is mainly concerned. Fortunately, for so far not much popularly written material has been published about them, especially when one considers the vast literature covering the history of the other branches of Judaism in the Diaspora.

The Western Sephardim sought and found refuge in Holland, but also in Southern France, Hamburg and England. The present work focuses mostly on the group that chose Amsterdam as its new fatherland. There they found peace, protection and the freedom to work and worship unhindered and unafraid. They not only contributed significantly to making Amsterdam the undisputed financial and commercial hub of the seventeenth and early eighteenth centuries Europe, they also created a vibrant Jewish religious and cultural centre that was to earn Amsterdam the name of 'The New Jerusalem'.

From Amsterdam, they then set out in the wake of the Dutch flag to help colonize the new Dutch territories in South America (Brazil), the Caribbean (Curaçao) and North America (New Amsterdam). They left behind a wealth of history that only in our times has become the subject of serious scientific research and historiography. Thus it is little wonder that the efforts to write about this branch of Judaism in a more popular form have been few and far between. Their number is even less when the story is told by a non-Jewish author and viewed through Christian eyes.

Piet Huisman's present work is such an exercise. In language that is understandable and meaningful to any lay reader, he tries to evoke these centuries of Jewish, but also Dutch, history. In doing so he does not limit himself to retelling the historic events; wherever necessary and useful to the non-Jewish reader he, inserts brief relevant background information.

The particular merit of Huisman's present effort lies in the retelling to a large audience a part of Jewish/Dutch and Dutch/Jewish history as enacted by a unique group of sometimes very ordinary, at other times truly visionary people. He thereby renders a welcome contribution to a better understanding between Christians and Jews.

Charles Gomes Casseres
President of the Consejo de Ancianos
of the Netherlands-Portuguese
Jewish Congregation
Mikve Israel-Emanuel of Curaçao.

Curaçao, November, 1986
at Curaçao, West-Indies.

A few years ago, Piet Huisman thought he had finished his studies of Jewish history and Sephardi cemeteries. His basic idea was that those who had made the history are still alive and among us. They live in the cemeteries, for instance in Beth Haim (House of the living) at Ouderkerk a/d Amstel in the Netherlands. Huisman then wanted to visit history itself, as materialized in Ets Haim (tree of life), the Sephardi Institute of Rabbinical Studies and the Library in Amsterdam.
Our meeting made clear that he still had a long way to go. And now he reaches the end of that road. Now there is his edition in the English language, showing his new approach of the subject and the influence of a few advisers. When a non-Jew achieves such a result on Jewish history, including trade, shipping and other relationships with all kinds of countries and people, it must be worthwhile to both Jewish and other readers. It also proves that the Jews belong to a world-wide system; that they cannot survive without the others and, not to forget, that the others owe very much to them. Of course, the author knew all this before, but now he offers many of those who did not realize this plain truth, a lesson. On the other hand, it remains a pity, that those who need the lesson most, will never learn.

D. L. Rodrigues Lopes,
Chairman of the Board of Governors
of Ets Haim, Amsterdam

12

Preface

On a hot Wednesday afternoon in October 1955, I wandered down to the old Jewish cemetery on the Island of Curaçao.
I had been stationed on this little island in the Caribbean some years before, and got interested in the relics of a not much described past, – that of the Jewish settlers in the South Americas.
The cemetery on Curaçao lies enclosed by an oil refinery. The bright unremitting sunlight threw a glare off the white weathered tombstones, echoed in the flashings of the oil pipes of the nearby refinery which hovered over the cemetery like a menacing shadow. As I stood watching, I was struck by how the remarkably carved tombstones, dating back to the seventeenth century, were slowly being swallowed by the ruthless advance of modern times.
It was thus both a sad and an impressive moment, for I made a decision then and there to prevent this piece of the past from dis-appearing forever. For certainly these stones won't be here much longer. The steady outpour of noxious gasses and the harmful smoke from the surrounding industry will see to that.
It's many years later now, and though sometimes it feels as though a lifetime has wedged itself between now and that sun-drenched afternoon in 1955, the original spell is still there. I guess one can carry these things within oneself without noting them very often only to have them return with even greater force.
I have gone back to that little cemetery, registering the decay of the stones, but also finding lots of information about the fate and life of the people that still figure in the relics. Names such as Cardozo, Maduro, Capriles, Henriques and Jacob-of-old-times ring with a curious old world exoticism that is particularly fascinating when encountered in the sub-tropics.
The Jews that lie buried in the Curaçao cemetery are of Sephardic heritage. The cemetery itself turns out to be the oldest Jewish cemetery of the Western Hemisphere. It seemed a good starting point. From here the journey goes forward and backward in time.
I decided to go backward first. I wanted to find out how these Sephardic Jews had gotten to this island. What had made them brave the seas in the early seventeen hundreds to eventually die in yet another strange land further than ever from their homeland?
And by what strange twists of logic had these ornamentations, so fitting in a Roman

Catholic setting but so utterly unfitting in a
Jewish context, come to adorn these age old
tombstones? The scenes that were carved in
the stones depicted scenes from the Bible,
explicit in their pictorial expression of life,
death and God.

These and other questions drove me back to
the source. I went to Israel. From there I
followed the quirky path that the Sephardic
Jews have followed in history, driven from one
place to another, searching for both religious
freedom and for social opportunities. It's this
journey that I present now in this book. It will
always remind me of that first encounter some
thirty years ago.

For you, the reader, I hope it will be an
introduction and possibly a renewed acquain-
tance with a spirit that has withstood the times.

Son, The Netherlands
September, 1986

The Ancient History

*Israel means 'fighter of the Lord'.
The patriarch Jacob got this name of
honour after his fight with the Angel
(Gen 23:2.91)*

The cradle of the Jewish people is situated in the Middle East, more specifically in the so-called Fertile Crescent. The area thus designated is formed by the head of the Persian Gulf from where it runs up the Valley of the Euphrates and south through what is now called Syria and Palestine to Egypt.

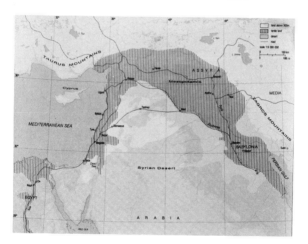

Although the history of Israel is commonly divided in five more or less distinct periods (pre-Israelic; First and Second Temple; diaspora; return and colonization and British mandate 'divide et empera'; declaration of the independant State of Israel), we will concern ourselves in this chapter for reasons of clarity and economy with the first three of those, the ancient history.

Pre-Israelic Period

We cannot say with any certainty that 'history begins at Sumer', but we can claim with reasonable accuracy that Jewish history begins there. It was out of this Sumer that the first Hebrews came, beginning with Abraham and his family. Probably not more than 4 million people – less than one thousandth of the world's present population – were alive in the year 10.000 BC. In the land of what was to become the land of Israel, whose present population is also about 4 million, fewer than

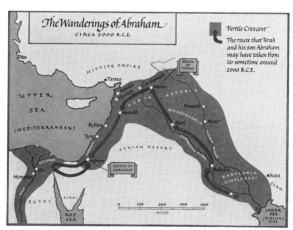

The Fertile Crescent: the land of Israel straddles the route from Mesopotamia to Egypt, giving it supreme importance as a commercial and cultural juncture.

100.000 people where living then according to the Biblical account, Abraham settled in Beersheba nearly 4000 years ago. The development of Mesopotamian city states around 3000 BC marks the emergence of Sumerian Civilization.

There is no doubt that the ceaseless warring first of city states, then of royal alliances, and finally of empires in the ancient Near East was a prime source of human suffering. Wars were waged for booty, slaves, raw materials, control of trade routes and imperial ambition. As a Sumerian proverb puts it: *'You go and carry off the enemy's land; The enemy comes and carries off your land'*

In a century of conquerors, no name looms larger than that of Sargon of Arkad. The Akkardians were of Semetic origin, and Sargon was also a Semite. The Akkardian dynasty founded by Sargon crumbled, but after the collapse of Akkad about 2180 BC the Sumerian city states regained much of their power. Prominent among these was Ur. After the reign of Ur-Nammu (ca 2100 BC) Ur also fell. It is at this point, about 2000 BC, with the advent of Abraham, that the history of the Jewish people begins. It is also called the Age of the Patriarchs.

For some centuries, until about the year 2000 BC, a group of nomads known as the Amurru, or Amorites, had been pressing on the settled cultures of Mesopotamia and Palestine. After the fall of the city of Ur, the great center of Mesopotamian culture, the Amorites (meaning 'Westerners') flooded the southern Mesopotamian plain. They adopted the culture of Sumer and the Akkadian language, which was the international commerce

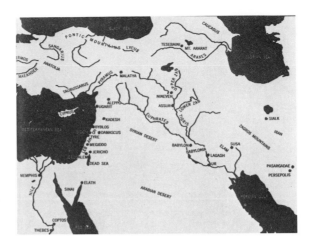

The ancient Near East.

language of that day. It is among these diverse clans of the 'Westerners' that the ancestors of Israel can be found.

They were herdsmen, their wealth was in sheep and goats and they moved often, from one pasture to another, from one waterhole to another. Their community was tribal, and their chief was the patriarch of the tribe. They lived in tents where they wove cloth from the wool of their beasts and worked leather from their skins. They worked copper into weapons and by trading wool or cheese, they acquired the knowledge to make bronze and used it for tools. Three and a half thousand years ago, there must have been hundreds of these tribes in the vast desert that stretches from the Red Sea to the Syrian highlands.

The tribes were linked into loose confederations, binding themselves to common if distant ancestors. We focus ourselves upon a singular group of tribes, who called themselves the Children of Israel, or the Bené-Yisrael. Exactly how many of these Children of Israel tribes there were is unknown. Although historians now speak of the Twelve Tribes as if this is a proven fact, it should be realized that the number 12 has long been considered magic. The Midianite tribal grouping was connected with the Israelites, for out of their tribe of Ken came Moses' bloodline. The Kenites were absorbed into the Israelite groups. Some hold that Abraham was an Amorite.

The Cannanites, with their black tents, made a name for themselves as the wanderers of the desert. They called them 'Hebrews' (the Ivrim, which means 'those who come from the other side of the river').

After many years important changes took place. First these tribes came in contact with the Hittites, a people of conquerors. From them, they acquired the knowledge of iron. Secondly, the horse appeared. Some hold that the Hittites brought them the chariot, about 1200 years before our era.

Amurru is the word for 'west' in Akkadian. It was also the Akkadian name for the unlikely land of Canaan. The land to which – out of the city of Haran – Abraham and his family came, pursuing, according to the Bible, a promise: *'Get thee out of my country, and from thy kindred, and from thy fathers house, unto a land that I will show thee: And I will make of thee a great nation' (Genesis 12:1-3)*

After this migration, which must have occurred after the Dynasty of Ur fell to the Amorites, Abraham moved his household southward to Schechem. Thereafter, when famine afflicted Canaan, they moved down to Egypt, and finally across the Sinai to Beersheba in the Negev.

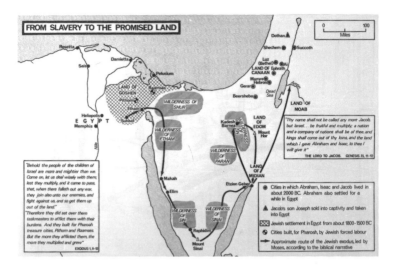

In Egypt (1900 BC) the Middle Kingdom was in its heydays. According to the evidence of the Egyptian Execration Texts (so-called because they list the enemies of Egypt) there appears to have been a resurgence of city life in Canaan during the 20th and 10th century BC, the period of Amorit absorption. In the time of Abraham several Amorite tribes settled down in Canaan and Mesopotania as farmers and traders. Some Amoritic tribes were slow to give up their semi-nomadic ways. Their number included Abraham and his descendants, the Patriarchs of Israel.

Both Christian and Moslem tradition view Abraham as their spiritual ancestor. To the Jews, he is the first patriarch, there being three patriarchs, e.g. Abraham, Isaac and Jacob. In the Hebrew tradition, Abraham is a man of faith; of a faith so profound that he was willing to sacrifice his son Isaac. But the biblical Abraham was also a man of the covenant through whom God was said to have forged a special link with the people of Israel. This

Detail of the frieze of the synagogue at Capernaum on the northern shore of the sea of Galilee. The synagogue, where Jesus delivered many of his discourses, was evidently destroyed by an earthquake.

covenant was later ratified as Moses stood on the mountain top in Sinai.

First and Second Temple

The Age of the Patriarchs ended with the descendants of Abraham setting out across the Sinai to their promised home. Israel had become an organic unity.

From this time onward, the Bible describes Israel as a separate nation with little reference to other cultures. The Israelites that came into Canaan were impregnated with Sumerian and Egyptian ideas. The difficulty with this aspect of Jewish history is the absence of any independent records. The number of Israelites who left Egypt was probably 600,000. The Bible tells us of no fewer than thirty-one Kingdoms that Joshua and the Israelites are said to have conquered. The 12th century land of Canaan presents a fascinating patchwork pattern: the Phoenicians (Sidonians) and Philistines along the Mediterranean coast and other tribes and people-Aramic, Moabit- and Ammonites spread around. In the interior, on both sides of the Jordan river, were the Israelites, the twelve tribes. The Philistines, however, were an economic as well as a continuing military threat to the Israelite tribes. After Saul, the first king of Israel, who was not very succesful in the ongoing battle against the Philistines, came King David. Under his reign and under his successor, King Salomon, the state of Israel was unified. Jerusalem was conquered and established as the focal point for the service to the God of Israel. The continuous attacks by hostile neighbor tribes were effectively quelled. King Salomon gave Israel its Golden Age. The spice trade with Arabia flourished, and his ships sailed to East Africa and India. Unfortunately, this time of prosperity

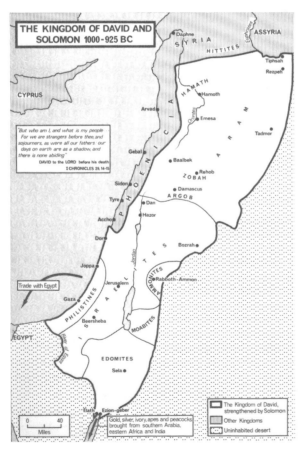

THE KINGDOM OF DAVID AND SOLOMON 1000-925 BC

"But who am I, and what is my people. For we are strangers before thee, and sojourners, as were all our fathers: our days on earth are as a shadow, and there is none abiding."
DAVID to the LORD before his death. I CHRONICLES 29.14-15

CYPRUS

SYRIA

ASSYRIA

Daphne

HITTITES

Tiphsah

Rezpeh

HAMATH

Hamoth

Arvad

Emesa

Tadmor

A
R
A
M

Gebal

Baalbek

Rehob

ZOBAH

Sidon

Damascus

ARGOB

Tyre

Dan

Accho

Hazor

Dora

Bozrah

Joppa

Rabboth-Ammon

Jerusalem

Trade with Egypt

Gaza

Beersheba

EGYPT

EDOMITES

Sela

Elath Ezion-geber

0   40
Miles

☐ The Kingdom of David, strengthened by Solomon
▨ Other Kingdoms
⬚ Uninhabited desert

Gold, silver, ivory, apes and peacocks brought from southern Arabia, eastern Africa and India

The Great Temple built by King Salomon which was meant to be the unified focus of Israelite worship and national identity. It was destroyed in 587 BC by the Babylonians.

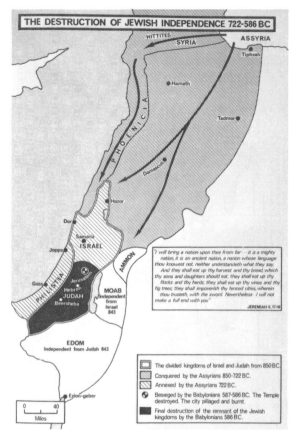

THE DESTRUCTION OF JEWISH INDEPENDENCE 722-586 BC

'I will bring a nation upon thee from far··· it is a mighty nation, it is an ancient nation, a nation whose language thou knowest not, neither understandeth what they say. And they shall eat up thy harvest and thy bread, which thy sons and daughters should eat; they shall eat up thy flocks and thy herds; they shall eat up thy vines and thy fig trees; they shall impoverish thy fenced cities, wherein thou trustedh, with the sword. Nevertheless- I will not make a full end with you"

JEREMIAH 6, 17-18

☐ The divided kingdoms of Israel and Judah from 850 BC.
◼ Conquered by the Assyrians 850-722 BC.
▨ Annexed by the Assyrians 722 BC.
✪ Besieged by the Babylonians 587-586 BC. The Temple destroyed, the city pillaged and burnt.
◼ Final destruction of the remnant of the Jewish kingdoms by the Babylonians 586 BC.

In 539 BC, Cyrus the Great conquered Babylon. In 538 BC, he issued a decree allowing the Jews to return to Jerusalem and rebuild the Temple. After a year a small group of Jews returned to the city of David.

In 520 BC, work on the Temple began anew. The Second Temple was completed in 515 BC, at which time Judea was no longer an independent Kingdom, but the sub-district of a Persian province. This lasted until 332 BC, when Alexander the Great, born in 356 BC, ruler of Macedonia, swept through Syria, Egypt and Palestine. After his death his empire was partitioned into two Hellenistic dynasties, the Ptolemies and the Seleucids. With the reign of Antiochus III and the Seleucid conquest of Judea, we stand on the verge of the Maccabean era and with it, the open conflict between Judaism and Hellenism. In 166 BC, Judah Maccabee ('Judah the Hammer') became the leader of the Jewish people and in 164 BC, reclaimed the Temple Mount in Jerusalem and rededicated the Temple (the festival of Hanukkah).

In 141 BC, the Maccabeans were in full control of Judea, and consolidated the dynasty of the Hasmoneans but the Hellenizing process continued. Some members of the Hasidim ('Pietist') joined Judea Maccabee. This group led the intellectual and political struggle against Hellenization. At the time, the Sadducees were the aristocrats in Judea, Organized around 200 BC, the Sadducees (from Zadok, the High Priest in the time of David and Salomon) were allied with the influencial priests that were, however, rather Hellenized. Opposed to them were the Pharisees. They were the spokesman for the people, and supported strict alliance to the

eventually ended. Internal strife led to a division of the Kingdom into two separate entities, Israel and Judea. Through cunning and deceit these two Kingdoms attempted to withstand the inevitable decay. Of the two, Judea lasted the longest until this Kingdom was also overrun by the Babylonians.
In 586 BC, Nebuchadnezar conquered Jerusalem and looted the city and burned down the Temple and palaces. Many leaders of Judea were executed and much of the surviving population was exiled to Babylon. Although Jews also went with Phoenician ships to Spain.

Under the Roman Commander Titus it took the Romans eight years to quell the rebellious Jews, but they eventually destroyed the Second Temple in Jerusalem and captured Masada in 74 AD.

Jewish law. The historian Flavius Josephus gives a description of the differences between Pharisees and Sadducees: *'Pharisees are friendly to one another and seek to promote concord with the general public, but the Sadducees even toward each other, show a more disagreeable spirit'.* Judea then knew a succession of kings that were in little or no respect remarkable. By persecuting the Pharisees, they drove the unstable kingdom right into the hands of the Romans, who at the time controlled the Mediterranean, Europe and North Africa. But the Judean political map knew two more specific population groups, the Essenes and the Zealots. Both groups eventually ceased to exist after reprisals by the Romans. During their existence, the Zealots opposed the appeasement policy of, specifically, the Sadducees. Struggles broke out among the polarized groups, and the Romans had to step in to preserve order. In 63 BC, Judea became a Roman province, ruled by obedient Jewish kings but closely watched by Roman governors. After the cruel reign of King Herod (37 BC-4 AD), the Romans decided not to allow the Jews any kings from their own ranks anymore. Roman procurators were installed to rule the land.

So all in all, the infighting among the diverse groups on the Judean scene had brought the participants disappointingly little. Perhaps from this frustration was born the last and dramatic uprising led by the aforementioned Zealots. They regarded the Roman rule as an insult to Jewish dignity. This time, however, the Romans decided to settle with these partisans once and for all. Under Titus, they devastated Jerusalem, burned the Second Temple, and slaughtered the riotous Jews by the ten thousands.

Like Nebuchadnezzar before him, Titus decreed that the survivors be sent into **exile** (90,000 were made slaves and scattered throughout the empire).

Diaspora

Jewish resistance did not end with the devastation of Jerusalem. Bands of Zealots held out in fortresses scattered throughout Judea, but nowhere longer than at Masada, overlooking the western shore of the Dead Sea. Led by Eleazar ben Yair, the Zealots had controlled the fortress since the early days of

The subjugation of the Jews was commemorated by the Romans through special coins bearing the inscription: 'Judea Capta'.

Exile

There was nothing unique about the suppression of a popular revolt by a people for the Romans, they did it also in other regions of their empire. And yet the defeat of the Jews seems to have inspired a special pride in the Roman commander Titus and his father, the Emperor Vespasian. They built a triumphal arch at the place where the Jewish captives bearing the menorah from the Temple were dragged into the Forum. In Jewish history, this is a turning point. It is the point from which the dominant theme of Jewish life is the diaspora, the condition of being dispersed, of being scattered. The Jews were to develop a special talent for living in diaspora. For being scattered and yet maintaining cohesion with each other. For being separated from their homeland and yet not forgetful of it. For being able to build autonomous centers of Jewish life under whatever government they happened to be living. The Diaspora begins with the events commemorated by the Arch of Titus. For a long period before, the Jews had been scattered far and wide throughout Babylonia and the Greek and Roman worlds. But from the time commemorated by the Arch of Titus, this becomes the central fact of Jewish History The era of wandering had now begun.

A Roman relief from the first century AD showing the plundering of the Temple.

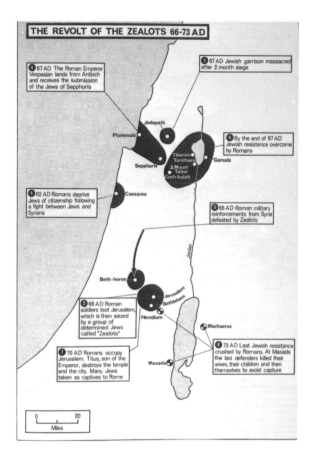

THE REVOLT OF THE ZEALOTS 66-73 AD

④ 67 AD The Roman Emperor Vespasian lands from Antioch and receives the submission of the Jews of Sepphoris

⑤ 67 AD Jewish garrison massacred after 2 month siege

⑥ By the end of 67 AD Jewish resistance overcome by Romans

③ 66 AD Roman military reinforcements from Syria defeated by Zealots

① 62 AD Romans deprive Jews of citizenship following a fight between Jews and Syrians

② 66 AD Roman soldiers loot Jerusalem, which is then siezed by a group of determined Jews called "Zealots"

⑦ 70 AD Romans occupy Jerusalem. Titus, son of the Emperor, destroys the temple and the city. Many Jews taken as captives to Rome

⑧ 73 AD Last Jewish resistance crushed by Romans. At Masada the last defenders killed their wives, their children and then themselves to avoid capture

Jodepath
Ptolemais
Tiberias
Tarichaea
Sepphoris
Mount Tabor
Gush-halab
Gamala
Caesarea
Jordan
Beth-horon
Jerusalem
Bethlehem
Herodium
Machaerus
Masada

0   20
Miles

of Masada, and set fire to a wooden barricade the Zealots had thrown together. At daybreak, when the Roman troops entered the fortress, they saw and heard nothing. They saw no sign of the enemy until, entering one of the buildings, they found the mounds of dead bodies, 960 in all. Men, women, and children. Only two women and five children survived.

Masada was the last stronghold where the rebellious Zealots held out to virtually the last man, woman and child. The fortress of Masada, situated atop a massive spur of rock overlooking the Dead Sea, was built by King Herod. It was an astonishing achievement, a testimony to the King's power, wealth and enterprise.

the Judean revolt in 66 AD, and had used Masada as a base for raids against the Romans. Not only did the rock fortress occupy a strong defensive position, with its fortified summit 1,300 feet above sea level, but King Herod had also installed a water system and storage facilities and living quarters. Many months passed before the soldiers of the Roman Tenth Legion, under the command of the Roman governor Flavius Silva, were able to erect a siege tower high enough to allow their iron battering ram to reach the fortress walls. But early in May of 73 AD, they breached the walls

The rest of Masada's defenders had chosen to commit suicide rather than submit to Roman captivity. To this resolve they were urged by the eloquence of their leader, Eleazar. The Masada excavations led by Yigael Yadin from 1963 to 1965 did uncover some circumstantial evidence lending credence to this story.
The Roman Emperors Vespasian and Titus thought so highly of their achievement in crushing the Jewish revolt that they had coins struck with the inscription 'Judea Capta'.

Within six decades after the fall of the Second

Temple, Israel had a new military leader, Simeon ben Kosiba (135 AD), or Bar Kokhba 'Son of the Stars'. The rebellion that Bar Kokhba would lead had it seeds in the decision by the Roman Emperor Hadrian (117-138 AD), to build over the ruins of Jerusalem a Roman City called Aelia Capitolina in his own honor, at the side of Herod's Temple. When the revolt broke out in 131/132 AD, the Roman Tenth Legion was forced to abandon Jerusalem. Under Bar Kokhba's leadership, a provisional government was established and plans were drawn up to rebuild the temple and resume the ritual sacrifices. A new calendar was proclaimed and new coins were issued. One such coin bears the inscription 'Shimeon (Bar Kokhba) President of Israel' on one side, and 'Year One of the Redemption of Israel' on the other.

Hadrian sent in reinforcements under Sextus Julius Severus. In 134/135 AD the Jewish rebels were driven from Jerusalem. Bar Kokhba was slain and his rebellion crushed. This marks a decisive break in Jewish history. At the time of the destruction of Jerusalem, more than half of all the Jews were not living in Judea. Many were living in **Babylonia** or in other parts of the Middle East and in various

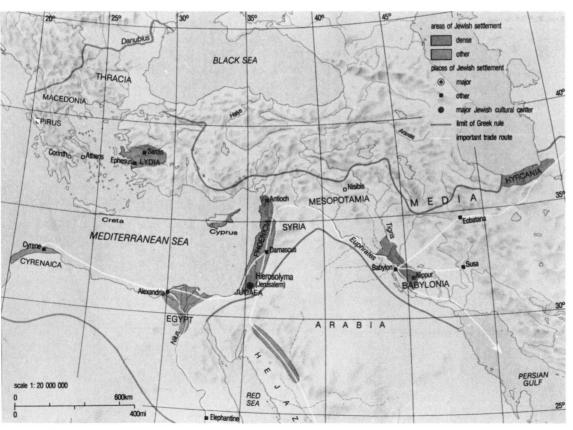

Babylonian and Jerusalem Talmud
The suppression of the Bar Kohba revolt marked an end to the supremacy of Judea in Jewish religious life. For the next several centuries, the leading centers of Jewish study and authority would be in Galilee and Mesopotamia. Reflecting this bifurcation is the fact that we have not one but two great compilations of Jewish law and learning-two versions of the Talmud. The Babylonian Talmud, vast in size and encyclopedic in scope, was compiled between 200 and 500 BC at Sura, Nehardea, Pumbeditha, and the other rabbinic academies of Babylonia, where Jews had lived continuously since Nebuchadnezzar had expelled them there. The second version is often called the Jerusalem Talmud, but this is a misnomer, since it was compiled predominantly in Caesarea, Tiberias and Sepphoris. About one-third the length of its Babylonian counterpart, the Jerusalem Talmud is accordingly less complete. Both versions of the Talmud have the same starting point, however, each takes the form of a commentary on the Mishna, which was codified in Galilee around 200 BC under the direction of Judah ha-Nasi (ca 217 BC). The redactors of the Mishnah, under Judah's leadership, saved for posterity not only the Oral Law (halakhah) but also the teachings of the rabbis (tannaim) during the first two centuries of the Common Era,

In 300 BC Jewish settlement still concentrated in the main in Judea and Babylonia, but new offshoots were blooming along the main trade routes and in the Greek cities.

when Rome twice laid waste to Judea. The disciples of Judah and their students (amoraim) would now provide an extended commentary on the work of their predecessors. This commentary, called Gemara, embraces not only halakhah but aggadah, e.g. the proverbs, parables, anecdotes and brief historical and biographical sketches that give the Talmud its principal literary interest.

A shekl from 67/68 AD found during excavations at Masada. It was minted to commemorate the first uprising of the Jews (66-70 AD).

communities of the Roman Empire. The later to be popularized legend of the **Wandering Jew** may have found its spiritual origins here. In time the Jews that had been forcibly evicted from their homeland learned to adapt to their new environments. From Italy they continued on to France, Russia (the Odessa) but especially to the Iberian peninsula. There they established themselves quite firmly, and grew to be a prosperous community. It would take a thousand years to see that the war with Rome, which ended with the expulsion of the Jews from their land, had paradoxically saved them from the fate that awaited other civilizations. For the Jews were exiled into survival.

The Wandering Jew
According to legend, Ahasverus was a shoemaker in Jerusalem. He refused to allow Christ, on his way to Calvary, to rest upon a stone. First mentioning of the Ahasverus legend was by a popular book, written in German and published in Leiden in the year 1602. The belief in the existence of 'Ahasverus, The Wandering Jew' was misused in the 16th and 17th centuries by many impostors. Goethe viewed this legend as the depiction of man who is deprived of a belief in something more exalted and continues his way through life, hesitatingly and grumbling. For other reasons, others consider Ahasverus as the representative of the Jewish people, dragging along their existence. Later on, he was considered as the symbol of the principle of Humanity (Hamelberg), or the free man challenging God (Shelley-Rochepin).

After the End

The Spanish era is one of the most extraordinary chapters in the history of the Jews. Although the exact date of the first settlement of Jews in Spain is unknown, there are many theories as to the time of their arrival. Some suppose they had been trading with the Iberians from the most distant times. Some historians, basing themselves on rabinical testimony of the 15th century, pinpoint the arrival in the days of Nebuchadnezzar, and possibly even before, in trading expeditions to the legendary Spanish Tarshish. Amador de los Rios believes their arrival was due to the stimulus of the trading expeditions of the Syrians and Phoenicians. The existence of Hebrew colonies together with Phoenician ones has been proven.

A Hebrew inscription found at Abdera (Adra), quoted by Father Mariana in his 'History of Spain', testifies that there were already Jews in the Peninsula in the 2nd and 3rd centuries. The inscription was found on the stone on the grave of a girl of little more than a year old, and it states that the child was Jewish. We presume that the motive for emigration of the Jews to the Iberian Peninsula was the end of Jewish Independence. The destruction of the second Temple in 70 AD and the tragic end of the revolt by Bar Kohba in 135 AD, brought many more Jewish fugitives to Spain. The descendents of these Jews are called **Sephardi Jews.**

During the Visigothik Monarchy

The Hebrews that fled from Jerusalem settled in North Africa and united themselves with the Vandals of Genseric. When their forces arrived in the south of the Peninsula, the Jews installed themselves in the new territories. In the beginnings of the dominion of the Visigoths, the Jews were well received and granted protection. The ruling Visigoths considered them useful to the economic ends of the Monarchy. The Arians were tolerant to them and with their aid, the Jews developed their ability for banking and economic affairs, enriching themselves and holding high positions in the Monarchy. Even their marriage with Christian girls was authorized.

During this Visigothic Monarchy, there existed three races in the Peninsula: Visigoths, Hispano-Romans and Jews. The fusion of the first two came to be complete, but the Jews always remained apart. Despite the efforts of several of the Visigothic kings to convert them to Christianity, the Jews put up a stubborn resistence. It is witnessed by the laws promul-

Sephardi Jews
The Jews of the oldest temples, used the word 'Sepharad' to indicate Spain. For the first time in the Bible, in the book Obadiah, the same as 'Tarshish' (tartessos) and 'Sarphat' (France). The oldest Syrian translation of the Bible (Pesito) translates 'Sepharad' as Spain. In biblical times 'Sepharad' was the indication for the Jews of the Western Overseas countries, colonized by the Phoenicians. Jonathan said in 'Targum', that many refugees from Jerusalem were living in the towns of the south of Spain. The biblical Jewish literature also identifies 'Sepharad' with Spain. In de Middle Ages 'Sepharad' was only indicated in connection with the Iberian Peninsula. That is why 'Sepharad' means: a Jew born in Spain.

gated to achieve this end: the 'Breviary' the 12th book of the 'Liber', the ordinances of the Councils of Toledo.

The Jews in the Visigothic epoch found themselves in a legal situation of inferiority compared with the other races. The 3rd Council obliged the children of unions between Christians and Jews to be baptized. King Sisebut faced such children with the dilemma: compulsory baptism or emigration. Later King Ervigio proposed to the 12th Council his 28 **anti-Jewish laws.** These included: absolute intolerance, compulsory recantation in the space of one year, confiscation, shaving of heads or flogging, both of Jews and of Judaizers aged more than ten, for any infraction.

King Egica decreed at the 17th Council that the Jews should be reduced to slavery and shared out among the Christians, who were expressly forbidden to free them. The tendency for their situation to worsen became evident as time went on.

The Synagogues were tolerated by the 'Breviary', but only those already built. Repairs and the construction of new ones were prohibited. Faced with the state of things, many Jews chose to be converted, but this appeasing attitude was hardly ever sincere. King Suintila annulled the anti-semitic laws.

Anti-Jewish laws
In face of the constant growth of the Jewish population, the Council of Illiberis decided to take measures. It decreed that they should live apart from the Hispano-Romans and forbade their marriage to Christian girls unless they were converted. A strict separation was also decreed between the Hispano-Roman race and the Semitic one, which was considered as impure. An attempt was made to prevent all kinds of intercommunication with its members, and it was even considered that the blessing of fields or crops, or any kind of goods, by the rabbis would attract all types of calamities. It was forbidden for a Christian to share the table with a Jew and the Christian who took a Jewess as his lover was anathematised.

A Jewish tombstone dating from 689 AD, around the time of the reign of the Visigoth King Egica.

On the one hand, the wish to separate them from public life became clearer, but on the other they did not want to lose them definitively, for they proved very useful to the Visigoths, a warlike people of great incapability in the practice of commerce.

The Moslem Domination

There is no doubt that the Jews cooperated in the Moslem invasion of 711. This is not surprising since they had suffered so much under the Visigoths. After the harsh measures taken by Sisebut, many had even emigrated to North Africa. When a Moor of Jewish blood, Tarik, penetrated Spain after the ruin of the Visigothic State, the Jews returned to Spain at the side of the Moslems.

It was then that a golden age began for the Spanish Jews. An age that lasted for more than three centuries. They settled in all parts of the peninsula and prospered. They were met by an atmosphere of tolerance – characteristic of the Arabs in their conquests – and the two religions, though irreconcilable, united against the symbol of the Cross. Under the shadow of the Crescent, the Israelites attained power, knowledge and riches.

Many Hebrews saw this turn of events as the rebirth of their race. They did not hesitate to dress as Arabs, to adopt their customs and language. The tolerance with which the Arabs treated them and the freedom which replaced the severe restrictions of the Visigoths, contributed to an even greater flourishing of trade and industry, especially after the establishment of the Caliphate, which incidentally, signalled the division of the Islamitic empire into two caliphates, the other residing in Bagdad. Under the Caliphate of Cordoba, the Jews placed themselves at the service of the Arab rulers. Rabbi Moses ben Henoch founded the Talmudic school of Cordoba. In Granada, the Jews lived in complete liberty, and several of them occupied prominent positions and performed diplomatic missions. Some cities were created and solely inhabited by Jews. One such city was Lucena.

Arab culture and Hebrew culture

The fact that Arabs and Jews lived peacefully together in Spain led to a brilliant culture. It was in Andalusia, the melting pot of races, where the most striking manifestations of this phenomena occured. The Hebrews reached impressive peaks of wisdom, learning and of artistic expression. Talmudic studies spread in the Spain of the Caliphate. The splendor of the Jewish schools in Moslem Spain was such that it eclipsed that of the Eastern ones.

In Spain, the Hebrew upper classes, much influenced by the Moslem culture, found themselves informed of their scientific knowledge: astronomy, medicine, botany and philosophy. The Moslem invasion, with all its historical and cultural consequences, influenced the eventual historical direction of Spain by its threat to the Christian world. This resulted in a rallying in the Christian-Roman world to the religious cause. Tensions became unavoidable.

With the coming of the Arabs, the strength of Judaism in the Peninsula became immensely reinforced. The tolerance which benefited them so much, however, was interrupted with the invasion of the Almoravides at the beginning of the 12th century. When the North African puritanical sect Almohades was summoned to the Peninsula in 1148 to check the threatening advance of the Christian kings who were constantly waging war from their states in the north of Spain, the reaction became drastic. The new rulers introduced to Spain the intolerance which they had already shown in Africa. Most of the Jews fled to the Christian kingdoms of the North. It is from this period that the hegemony of the communities of Christian Spain may be said to date. Large numbers of the Jews that stayed put were killed or sold into slavery by the ruthless Moslem sect. A minority, however, outwardly embraced the religion of Islam. In their hearts they remained steadfast. On the other hand, large parts of Jews paid lip service to the Christian faith, but in the privacy of their homes stayed faithful to the traditions of Judaism. In the African possessions of the Almohades, the recent Jewish converts were ordered to wear a distinguishing sign. Among the victims of the Almohadan persecution was Rabbi Maimon, who left Cordova with his family after a period of wandering and found refuge in Fez. Here, Maimon wrote his famous Letter of Consolation.

The Origins of Marranism

The Reconquest, or Reconquista, in Spain put additional pressure on the Jews. The Christian kings could not easily distinguish between unbelievers and believers. Besides that, the Jews dressed in the same fashion as the Moslems and spoke their language. They therefore also shared their fate. Mosques and synagogues alike were burned and Jewish and Islamitic populations put to the sword.
As the Reconquest progressed, the situation for the Jews in the Hispanic Kingdoms became increasingly difficult. The laws decreed by the Castilian monarchs restricted their constitutional rights more and more. The converts ('*Marranos*') were spared the anti-Jewish legislation. This did not prevent a general hostility towards them. The pretender of the throne, Henry, professed a deep loathing for the Israelites and accused Peter I of being a Judeophile.

In 1212, the Christian kings, aided by knights from Europe, dealt the Moslims a decisive blow at the Battle of Las Navas de Tolosa and their power was finally crushed. This event synchronized with the promulgation of the anti-Jewish-policy which had been enunciated

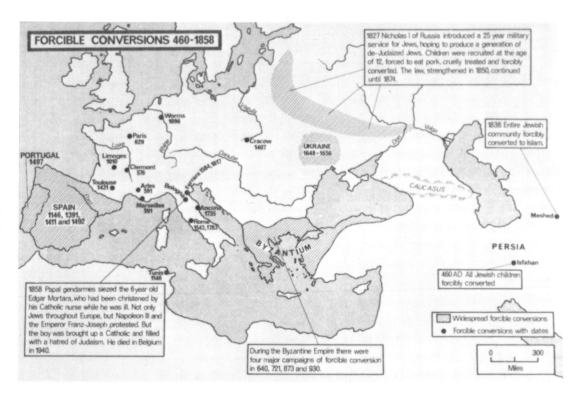

FORCIBLE CONVERSIONS 460-1858

1827 Nicholas I of Russia introduced a 25 year military service for Jews, hoping to produce a generation of de-Judaized Jews. Children were recruited at the age of 12, forced to eat pork, cruelly treated and forcibly converted. The law, strengthened in 1850, continued until 1874.

1838 Entire Jewish community forcibly converted to Islam.

1858 Papal gendarmes siezed the 6 year old Edgar Mortara, who had been christened by his Catholic nurse while he was ill. Not only Jews throughout Europe, but Napoleon III and the Emperor Franz-Joseph protested. But the boy was brought up a Catholic and filled with a hatred of Judaism. He died in Belgium in 1940.

During the Byzantine Empire there were four major campaigns of forcible conversion in 640, 721, 873 and 930.

460 AD All Jewish children forcibly converted

Widespread forcible conversions

● Forcible conversions with dates

0   300
Miles

PORTUGAL 1497

SPAIN 1146, 1391, 1411 and 1492

Paris 629

Limoges 1010

Clermont 576

Toulouse 1431

Arles 591

Marseilles 591

Tunis 1146

Worms 1096

Cracow 1407

UKRAINE 1648-1656

Bologna 1554, 1817

Ancona 1735

Rome 1543, 1783

BYZANTIUM

CAUCASUS

PERSIA

Isfahan

Meshed

by the Lateran Councils of 1179 and 1215. In the financial administration of the country, individual Jews continued however to enjoy considerable influence. In October 1390, Juan I of Castile died. He was succeeded by his infant son Henry III (1390-1406). The confessor of the Queen Mother Leonora, Archdeacon, Ferrand Martinez, became a power figure in the state. He was a sworn enemy of the Jews. By letters to the local clergy, he procured the destruction of some of the unauthorized Jewish places of worship. His sermons steered the popular hostility towards the Jews to the highest pitch. On June 4, 1391, the mob could no longer be restrained. The Juderia of Sevilla was sacked. As many as four thousand Jews were killed, while those who could not escape were able to save their lives only by accepting baptism. The fury spread through the whole of the Peninsula, from the Pyrenees to the straits of Gibraltar. At Carmona, the whole community was exterminated. At Cordova, the entire Juderia was reduced to ashes. At Barcelona, the whole Jewish community was wiped out.
In 1355 and 1391, the mercenary troops of Henry II invaded **Toledo**; a thousand Jews were massacred and synagogues were destroyed. The tension between the Marranos (converted Jews) and the religious authorities continued to increase.

Such waves of massacres were not new in Jewish history. Something of the sort had taken place in the Rhineland during the Crusades; in England in 1189-1190; and Germany during the period of the Black Death. Here the vast majority of victims had unquestioningly preferred martyrdom, rather than abjure their faith.

But in Spain conditions were different. The morale of the people had been undermined by centuries of well-being. Their social assimilation to the general population had progressed so far as to make the change seem perhaps less drastic. The expulsions throughout Europe (from England in 1290; from France in 1306 and 1394; from the majority of the cities of Germany at the time of the Black Death) had cut off most avenues of escape. But, above all, there was a moral difference, which had been shown in the long tradition of crypto-Judaism in the Peninsula. Such being the reasons, throughout the Peninsula, large bodies of Jews accepted baptism in order to escape death.
The total number of **conversions** in the Kingdoms of Aragon and Castile is estimated to be two hundred thousand. This is a unique phenomenon in the whole of Jewish history. Of the neophytes, some returned to Judaism when the immediate danger was past, fleeing for that purpose to parts of the country where they were unknown, or else to Moslem Africa. From the close of the 14th century, a complete new state of affairs existed in Spain. At the side of those who still openly professed their Judaism, were vast numbers of Marranos (conversos, crypto-Jews), totaling some hundreds of thousands in all. At heart they remained as Jewish as they had ever been. Their disbelief in the dogmas of the Church was notorious. They kept all the traditional ceremonies. In race, in belief, and largely in practice, they remained as they had been before the conversion. They were Jews in all but name, and Christians in nothing but form. The social and economic progress of the Marranos and their descendants developed

Toledo-the Jerusalem of the Sephardic Jews
Toledo was the ancient capital of Castile. Its Jewish community is the oldest in Spain and under the Visigoths was the most important in Spain. It flourished under Moslem rule, and was a Karaite center. In the 14th century it had nine Synagogues, and two of these are still standing. Like the ancient city of Jerusalem, Toledo stands on a height, surrounded by little villages. It is encircled by the river Tagus. Toledo was an outstanding cultural center. Abraham Aben David (1110-1180), author of the famous 'Book of Tradition', the first complete chronicle of Judaism, was a Toledan. So was the poet Juda Halevi, whose great philosophical works are the 'Cuzari' and 'The Confessions'. The Jewish

very rapidly. It was now out of the question to exclude them from any walk of life on the ground of their creed. The Law, the Administration, the army, the universities, the Church itself, were all overrun by recent converts or by their immediate descendants. They all but dominated Spanish life. The wealthier of the converts intermarried with the highest nobility of the land. Within a couple of generations, there was barely a single aristocratic family in Aragon or Castile, from the royal house on downwards, which was free from the 'taint' of Jewish blood.

Important figures of the fifteenth century were: Solomon ha Levi, alias Pablo de Santa Maria, Bishop of Burgos. His son Alfonso, also became a Bishop and was one of the Spanish delegates to the Church Council of community was hit hard by the 1391 massacres and thereafter was a Marrano center. The Inquisition was active in Toledo from 1486. The Jews left with the expulsion from Spain in 1492.

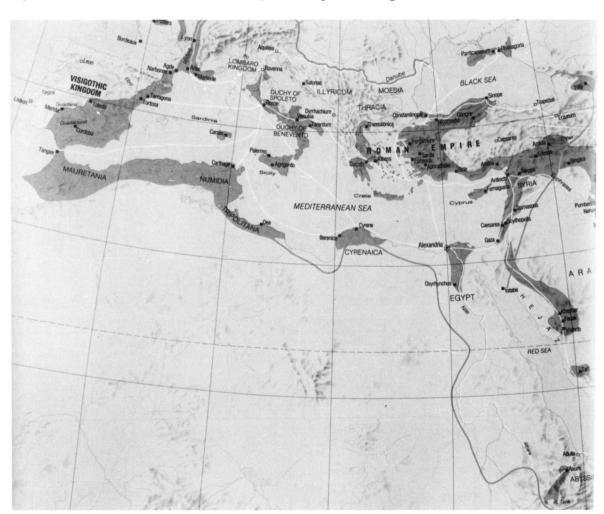

Around 600 AD, Christianity has been well established in the area of the old Roman empire. Jewish settlements in Western Europe have grown significantly, but the most important area with a Jewish population is still Babylonia.

The myth of conversion
The Jews who were compelled by circumstances to adopt Christianity often only outwardly did so. Secretly, they followed Jewish rites and customs. These crypto-Jews were called Marranos, the word meaning 'swine' in Spanish; the Hebrew 'anusim' meaning 'forced ones'. Elsewhere the Marranos are called New Christians. Marranos became a significant factor after the anti-Jewish massacres of 1391 in Spain, when many Jews adopted Christianity to escape death. Knowing that many continued secretly as Jews, the Inquisition was introduced to ferret out such cases. It was directed against the Marranos in the Iberian Peninsula and later against their descendants in Latin America; tens of thousands were burned at the stake. Descendants of Marranos have been discovered in Portugal and South America still observing Jewish customs, but without knowing the reasons.

Basle, the anti-Jewish policy of which he advocated. His brother Gonzalo was Bishop of Sigüenza. The Cardinal of San Sisto was Juan de Torquemada, a man of immediate Jewish descent.

The Lunas, Mendozas, Villahermosas and others of the proudest nobility contracted family alliances with wealthy conversos. So did the Henriquez family to which the mother of Ferdinand the Catholic belonged. At least seven of the principal prelates of the Kingdom were of Jewish extraction, as well as the contador mayor, or Treasurer. There was hardly a single office of importance at either court, especially in the financial administration, which was not occupied by the descendants of some converted Jew or by members of his family.

In intellectual life, conditions were similar. Hernando de Pulgar Andres Heli, Pedro Guttierez de Santa Clara, Fernando de Rojas were famous writers. A well-known poet of Jewish blood was Rodrigo Cota da Maguaque. Francisco Lopez de Villalobos was one of the classical writers in the Spanish tongue and one of the most famous physicians of his time. In the arts, Juan de Levi, a religious painter at the beginning of the 15th century, and Juan de Altabás were of Jewish descent.

The Expulsion from Spain and Portugal

A distinct and ominous chapter in the history of the Jews in Spain and, later, Portugal is formed by the establishment of the **Inquisition.** Although by no means exclusive to the Iberean Peninsula, the Spanish Inquisition gained a fearful reputation as it reached notorious heights in its persecution of heretics, the Jews being the most important. It played at least as important a role in the inevitable decline of Spanish Jewry as did the successive decrees and bans by Visigoths, Moslem and Christian rulers before them.

The Inquisition had a widespread field of action. From the South of France it extended all over Europe. The three countries where its activities had the greatest importance were Italy, France and Spain. In France it gradually fell into disuse and no one was executed for heresy after the second half of the 18th century. In Italy, Pope Paul II created the Roman Inquisition in 1543. In Portugal, King John II requested the establishment of the Inquisition.

In Spain, during its first period, the Inquisition was confined to the Kingdom of Aragon, specifically in its Trans-Pyrenean territories. At first the Bishop of Tarragona was entrusted with its foundation, and it was then continued by the Dominicans.

Racial definition

The Inquisition was set up in Spain according to the canonical norms in 1237, but did not begin to function until the 15th century. The Spain of 1391, which spawned the first great wave of New Christians, had not yet developed a racial definition of 'Jews' to encompass Catholics of Jewish descent. The Spanish Marranos entered Catholicism and Christian society vigorously and enthusiastically, quickly penetrating the ranks of the Castilian middle and upper classes and occupying the most prominent positions in the royal administration and the Church hierarchy.

The hostility of the masses to the marranic elite led first, around the middle of the 15th century, to the notorious **'Purity of Blood Statutes'**, and then, in the early 1480's, to the establishment of the Spanish Inquisition. When the need to install the Inquisition in Spain originally had come up, it was met with little enthusiasm by the Catholic sovereigns. Queen Isabella, though, while originally being rather benevolent towards the Jews, recognized in the institution of the Inquisition a means of solidifying her power. Like Louis IX of France, John II of Portugal and Henry VIII of England, she had to struggle against the

The Inquisition
The Inquisition was a Catholic ecclesiastical tribunal dealing with the detection and punishment of heresy. At first it dealt only incidentally with Jews, but from 1478, it was established in Spain to deal with Marranos. The first of the tribunal's actions took place in February 1481 when six converts or so-called Marranos were burnt to death. The auto-da-fé ('act of faith') was to become a regular spectacle. At least 2,000 autos-da-fé were held, in almost all of which persons of Jewish descent were featured. From the institution of the Inquisition to the death of Torquemada, the first head of the Spanish Inquisition who was appointed in 1483, 10,000 Jews were condemned to the stake. Furthermore, 6,600 who fled were burnt in effigy and 97,000 were condemned to the penalty of infamy, confiscation of goods or life imprisonment. It should be noted that the Inquisition had no jurisdiction over Jews but only those Jews who had embraced Christianity and were suspected of observing Judaism in secret. Over 350 years, some 400,000 persons were tried by the Inquisition in Spain and Portugal on charges of being secret Jews or influencing others to keep Jewish observances, and some 30,000 were put to death.

Purity of Faith and Purity of Blood
'Purity of faith' was worth as much for the Spaniard of the great centuries as purity of blood. Purity of blood was a cause of legitimate pride among the Castilians. The medieval Code – so-called the 'Partidas' – defined 'Hidalguia' as 'the nobility which

31

nobility in order to unify power.

The Holy office aspired to be a purely ecclesiastical court, inspired by the highest principles of Christian doctrine. It tried to obtain the repentance of the condemned in order to save their souls, and to work mercifully. It had no executioners; these were the officials of the State, and they executed no sentence. Later, things began to change gradually. It acted on the basis of 'the canons against heretics, Moors and Jews who are apostates to the faith'.

Although at first the Inquisition's activities were confined to the purely religious sphere, they soon extended to the whole of civil life. Bigamy, smuggling, political activities or immoral literature were judged just the same as the religious transgressions of members of the Church. Thus it soon became the terror of practicing Jews, who should have been excluded from its action by virtue of its own constitution. Thus the Tribunal of the Inquisition was no longer subject to the Pope but to the Spanish clergy, and the inquisitors were appointed by the sovereigns. The creators of the new institution were Thomas de Torquemada, the Queen's confessor and Prior of the Dominican monastery of the Holy Cross at Segovia (whose mother, incidentally, was of Jewish lineage), and Archbishop of Seville, Mendoza, an inveterate enemy of the Marranos.

The established Marranos soon saw in the Inquisition a serious danger and hastened to oppose it. The delegates of Torquemada began acting through the use of edicts. A comes to men through lineage'. The man who inherited a lineage of hidalguia through the paternal line was noble. The mother's lineage also counted, but on a secondary plane, for it was subjected to the status of the male. Purity of blood was as important as honor, which was the greatest of man's goods on this earth, whereas riches and material goods were regarded as perishable things. Thus any kind of blemish in the whiteness of a noble lineage, however remote it might be, was perpetual and ineffaceable. It was not enough for a Jew to be three quarters hidalgo or 'Old Christian', for only a small part sufficed to affect him.

In Castille and Aragon, it was difficult to find a noble family that was not connected with Hebrew families. King Ferdinand the Catholic descended from the convert Enriquez on his mother's side; while the uncles of Torquemada himself came from Jewish stock, like the descendants of Alfonso V of Aragon. Other descendants of converts were Ferdinand de Rojas, St. Teresa of Jesus and the Blessed John of Avila.

In the Orders of Chivalry the very strict statute of purity reigned. According to the constitutions of the Order of Santiago of 1573, admittance was refused to any person who had the blood of a Jew, Moor or Marranos on the side of the father, mother or in any degree, however remote it might be. The descendants of those condemned for heresy were disqualified down to the 4th degree.

The Inquisition acted on the basis of 'the canons against heretics, Moors and Jews who are apostates to the faith'. In lenghtly and sometimes bizarre manifestations, known as 'Auto da Fé', many were burned alive.

group of militants under the Marranos tried to protest, but no notice was taken of them, so they resolved to take justice into their own hands. In Sept. 1485, the inquisitor Pedro Arbués was murdered. The reaction was swift and terrible. The converts of Saragossa became the object of the people's wrath, while many Jews of high ranks were also murdered. The Spanish Inquisition of the 16th century was in its fundamentals a new body, different from the medieval one of the 13th century. The latter was exercised by an ecclesiastical Tribunal appointed by the Pope. Now the State took over the functioning. Pope Paul III – through the Bull 'Licet ab Initio' – sanctioned it as a body to act against the Protestant heresy. Pope Sixtus IV censured the procedures of the Inquisition in a Bull. The flames burned around the stakes from Cordoba, to Jaen and from Ciudad Real to Toledo. The Inquisition was instructed to impose a clear distinction between Christians and Jews. It was not only directed against the supposed heretics of the Marranos, but also against all suspect Catholics. Nobody was safe from the

Inquisition. It had at its disposal refined instruments for torture, prescribed in detail by the 'Compilation' of Torquemada.

The Expulsion

In spite of all the activities of the Inquisition, the Catholic Sovereigns and the Inquisitor Torquemada found themselves faced with a problem, the solution of which grew more and more urgent. The entire people – spurned on by ungrounded malicious rumors such as the **Blood Libel** – were clamoring for the disappearance of the race that had installed itself so firmly in Spanish territory. There remained no other formula than expulsion to put an end to the 'Jewish peril', for the pogroms had shown clearly that the Jews could not be drowned in their blood. Also, King Ferdinand and Queen Isabella considered the Jews a source of disunity for the kingdom and of contamination for the *conversos*, who, after all, were suspected of embracing Christianity insincerely. It was felt that these Marranos were using the immunity and privileges to work against the Catholic fate. When it was thus realized that they were hardly ever sincere, they were considered a potentially dangerous element.

After having condemned tens of thousands to death or infamy, the Inquisition under Torquemada thus decided to have the problem removed from them. The consequent expulsion that was largely orchestrated by Torquemada put an abrupt and in many ways tragic end to many centuries of Jewish presence in Spain. It had evolved from a prosperous community, contributing heavily to the advancement of commerce, medicine and literature, to a persecuted group in a

The blood libel
Toward the middle of the twelfth century – as Christian Europe braced itself for the Second Crusade – the rumor began to spread that at Passover time Jews murdered Christian children in order to use their blood in the preparation of the matzah, the unleavened bread. The first documented instance of this 'blood libel' (which probably has its roots in pre-Christian times) appears in 'The Life and Miracles of Saint William of Norwich', written about 1173 by a Benedictine monk, Thomas of Monmouth. In 1144, according to Thomas' writing, the hero of his tale, a young boy called William, was taken captive by the Jews of Norwich, tortured and put to death, in mockery of the Crucifixtion. The allegation that Jews sought Christian blood was mendaciously ascribed to nonexistent pages in the Torah and the Talmud. There is no single passage in the Torah or Talmud, or any other Jewish writing, that calls for the shedding of non-Jewish blood. But truth is never a complete impediment to rumor. This blood libel surfaced on the continent at Blois, France, in 1171, and at Saragossa, Spain, eleven years later.

The expulsion from Spain put an end to many centuries of Jewish presence in Spain.

THE JEWS OF SPAIN AND PORTUGAL 1000-1497

Jews played a leading part in the cultural and economic life of Spain during the Roman, Islamic and Christian periods. Many were converted to Christianity in the 100 years before the expulsion. Jews were active in most occupations, and are known to have been doctors, lawyers, carpenters, tailors, butchers, bookbinders, tax-collectors, moneylenders, candlemakers, shipowners, sheep farmers, horse dealers and even lion-tamers. Jewish merchants dealt in silk, grain, furs, leather, wool and timber

1228. Jews forced to wear distinctive badge

1355. 12,000 Jews massacred by the mob

1391. 50,000 Jews killed

1373, 1449, 1482. Anti-Jewish riots

1492 Expulsion
To Turkey	90,000
To Holland	25,000
To Morocco	20,000
To France	10,000
To Italy	10,000
To America	5,000
Total emigrated	160,000
Died while seeking a new home	20,000
Baptized, and remained in Spain	50,000

• Towns with Jewish communities by 1490
◉ Anti-Jewish massacres 1391-1397
← The expulsion of the Jews 1492-1498

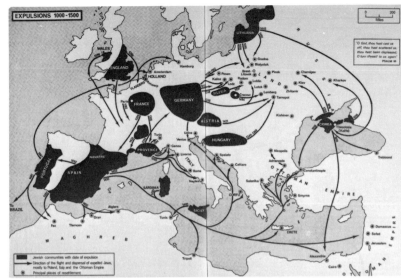

EXPULSIONS 1000-1500

'O God, thou hast cast us off, thou hast scattered us, thou hast been displeased; O turn thyself to us again.'
PSALM 60

■ Jewish communities with date of expulsion
→ Direction of the flight and dispersal of expelled Jews, mostly to Poland, Italy and the Ottoman Empire
◉ Principal places of resettlement

hostile society. Yet the expulsion order that in 1492 was directed against them did much to upset their already shaken confidence. It has been pointed out before that expulsions of Jews had taken place before 1492, notably in England in 1290, three times in France during the fourteenth century and in Germany from 1348 to 1350. It is safe to assume that the current victims of expulsion knew about these previous ones, and therefore had no safe destination once they left Spain.

Reflecting this concern of the 100,000 or more Jews who left Spain after King Ferdinand and Queen Isabella signed the edict of banishment on March 3, 1492, the majority went to Portugal. There was at this time a relatively flourishing community in Portugal that was ruled by King John II (1455-1495).

There were other Jews that tearfully left the Iberean Peninsula altogether, leaving behind the graves of their ancestors and with that a large part of their social and cultural history.

Harassed on their way, they made it to Italy and Germany, while others went to Salonica, Alexandria, Venice, Naples and dominions of the Turkish Empire. With the favorable exception of the Papal States and Turkey, the refugees did not meet much of a welcome from the states that had only shortly before publicly criticized the 'unjust and cruel measure' of expulsion to which the Jews had fallen victim. Different numbers are given for the actual number of Jews that eventually left Spain. They range from 160,000 to 300,000. It has been estimated that the Jewish population at the time of the expulsion order totaled around 400,000.

It should be born in mind that the expulsion order took a relatively long period to carry out. Furthermore, the Spanish authorities did not enforce the actual leaving of Jews that had risen to high and valuable positions right away. These Jews were for a time considered 'productive' and a policy of replacement of these particular individuals had to be implemented before they too were forced to leave. Once considered no longer valuable to the interest of the Spanish state these remaining Marranos stood in the immediate danger of falling into the hands of the Inquisition. The new arrivals in Portugal had to pay for their relative security. King John II taxed the wealthier Jews 100 cruzados for the right of permanent residence in his kingdom. Poorer Jews paid 8 cruzados a head for a stay of up to eight months. When this period came to an end they were given the choice between conversion to Christianity or banishment from the land. Much more threatening developments were, however, on the way.

In 1496, King John's successor, Emanuel I (1495-1521), contracted a dynastic marriage with Princess Isabella, the latter a daughter of King Ferdinand and Queen Isabella of Spain. As a precondition for this rational royal match, the Catholic sovereigns – with whom Queen Isabella was struggling over the political power – insisted that Emanuel I rid Portugal of its Jews, many of whom had arrived there since 1492. On December 4, 1496 the required expulsion decree was issued. But Emanuel I was reluctant to see the economic factor that the Jews had come to represent actually leave his country. He therefore sought to forcibly baptize all minor Jews, a measure that took place on March 19, 1497. However, the defacto annexation of Portugal to the Spanish Crown broadened the spread of operations by the Inquisition. In 1497, five years after the expulsion from Spain, a massive outpouring of Jews from Portugal took place. A by all means unique chapter in their history had come to a most definite close.

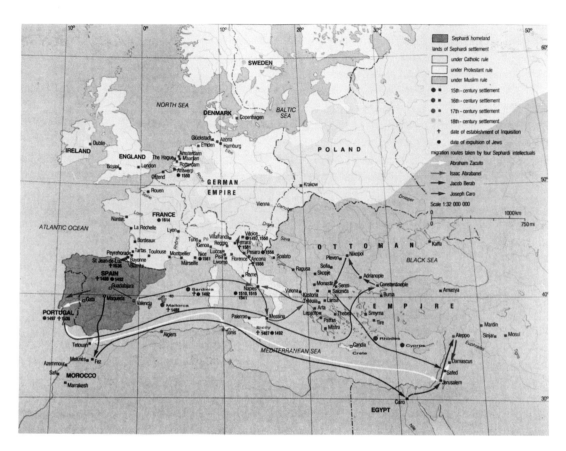

The Sephardi diaspora, c. 1500-1700 AD. The map traces in detail the wanderings of four refugees from Spain, all famous scholars: Abraham Zacuto, Isaac Abrabanel, Jacob Berab and Joseph Caro.

The Low Countries

The expulsion of Jews from Spain, and the subsequent chain of events that allied Spain and Portugal closely together made the living circumstances for the Portugese Jews (including those that had fled from Spain) a precarious one. It was clear that, notwithstanding King Emanuel's I relatively moderate stance, they could not safely remain. Many of the Jews took to the road in much the same directions as the expelled Jews from Spain had taken before them: they went to the Low Lands. At the same time, refugees from Portugal also went to Palestina where they settled in the town of Safed (in Galilee) which was to become a center of study and mysticism. With them came the curious blend of Spanish and Hebrew that was the basis for their language, **Ladino**.

Brewing conflicts

The lands the Jews made their way to were embroiled in a number of conflicts. The accession of Charles V brought the Netherlands – or the so-called 17 provinces – into the huge and incongruous collection of states which the wars and marriages of the Spanish royalty and the Hapsburgs had heaped together. Both religious and secular conflicts broke out with a disturbing regularity. These chain of events led to formidable riots in many places, especially Antwerp, during which images, altars, pictures and stained glass windows of the churches were smashed. The Duchess of Parma, Margaret, ordered the insubordination of the Protestants to be quelled. The veteran Spanish general, the Duke of Alva, was already on his way from Italy with a force of about 10,000 men.

FERDINANDUS ALVARES TOLETANUS DUX ALVÆ
nomine Regis in gubernatione secundus ab anno 1567 ad
annum 1574 imperavit.

Fernando Alvarez de Toledo, Duke of Toledo (1508-1583), a descendant of one of the most illustrious families in Spain. In 1567, he was sent to the Netherlands to repress Protestantism there.

Ladino
The Jews of Spanish origin spoke a Judeo-Spanish dialect that spread around their communities in the eastern Mediterranean areas. Its basis is medieval Castilian, but there is an admixture of other languages, including Hebrew, Greek, and Turkish. It is written in Hebrew letters. Literature in Ladino was written from the Middle Ages and contains much folk poetry, as well as works on religious and ethical subjects. From the 18th century newspapers and novels were also written. It was widely spoken in Balkan countries but was on the decline before World War II. This decline was hastened by the events during the war and the emigration of most Balkan survivors to Israel, where Ladino is still spoken and read but its usage confined increasingly to the older generation.

So it was anything but a safe haven the Jews had reached when they first settled in Antwerp, Middelburg and Flushing. Antwerp especially turned out to be a pivotal location as here was the center of trade with the Spanish empire as well as a hot spot for political and religious discontent. Charles V intended to expell the Jews just as they had been expelled from Spain itself. A mandatory registration of the Jews that were present and a limit on the Jews that entered was ordered. (This was, incidentally, most certainly not the first time that the escaped Jews from Spain and Portugal felt the screws tighten again. In 1549, for example, an edict was issued expelling from the Low Countries all new Marranos arriving from Portugal during the last five years. The Burgomasters of Antwerp resisted and refused to sign the edict. However, in 1550 the regulation was enforced).

Some of the well-known families that were

PHILIPPVS, II. AVSTRIACVS HISPANIARVM INDIARVM NEAP. HIEROSOL. REX.

established in Antwerp at the time betrayed in their name their marrano descent, such as the trading house of the family Ximenez and the family Mendoza. Donna Mencia de Mendoza was given in marriage to Count Henry of Nassau at Breda by the emperor Charles V. The coming of General Alva inspired fear in the Jews of Antwerp. Soon after his arrival, Margeret the Duchess of Parma resigned as Governor-General of the 17 provinces, a post that she had filled for King Philip II.

Alva's rule from 1568 to 1573 is a great example of military despotism. He was the indisputed master in the Netherlands and settled down to the military, ecclesiastical, judicial and other measures which were needed to consolidate his success. One such measure was the imposing of the infamous tax, the so-called Tenth Penny on all personal property, and the Twentieth Penny on the sales of all real estate. The reasoning behind these tremendously unpopular and consequently sabotaged measures was that the Spanish Crown could no longer afford to pay its troops in Holland. The tax was therefore introduced to pay them and to prevent mutiny under the soldiers.

The departure of Marranos from Antwerp and the subsequent loss of work for many seamen coincided with a phenomena in every other respect much removed from the fate of the Sephardi Jews. The seamen thus out of work took up with the followers of William the Silent who was waging war on Alva to liberate the Netherlands, and who had granted some of his followers commissions to act as privateers. These fierce sea rovers – nicknamed *Gueux de mers* or in Dutch *Geuzen* – seized on April 1, 1572 the port of Brill, at the mouth of the

Alva united Catholics and Protestants against him when, in desperate need for money, he attempted in 1569 to Levy a property tax and a 10% turnover tax on all sales.

King Philip II, King of Spain (1527-1598). External and internal influences alike drove Philip into conflict with the Netherlands, France and England.

Maas. Soon after this they took Flushing, which commands the other great waterway, the Scheldt. Within three months of the capture of Brill, Amsterdam was the only town still remaining to the Spaniards in the province of Holland. As battle raged throughout the provinces, a new element was making its appearance in history: the burghers began to show a heroism with which the Spaniards could not cope. At Alkmaar victory began; the dikes were cut and the Spanish armies had to withdraw before the advancing inundations. Finally in October, Alva's fleet was defeated and the general left Brussels on December 18, 1573.

The multifacetted events that followed the initial success for the rebels are too involved to be treated here at length. The upshot, however, of the struggle for freedom by the northern provinces from Spanish domination clashed with the growing fear of the southern provinces for the growth of Calvinism. Underpaid and mutinious Spanish troops settled in Alost from where they marched on Antwerp on October 3, 1576. Called the Spanish Fury, the troops overpowered the garrison and sacked the greatest city of the Netherlands with barbarous ferocity. The return of the Spanish led to a renewed departure of Jews remaining in Antwerp. Their destination was clear, the northern provinces which had as good as won their independence and were to maintain it as a republic.

The Sephardi Community

The first evidence of organized Jewish religious life in Amsterdam dates from the beginning of the seventeenth century, when services were held on Joncker Street. It has been assumed that nearly ten years earlier, in 1593, religious Jews from Spain or Portugal had held prayer meetings in Amsterdam. In

On April 1st, 1572 a small outfit of privateers, acting on behalf of William of Orange, captured the port of Brielle.

The Portuguese Synagogue in Amsterdam built in 1675.

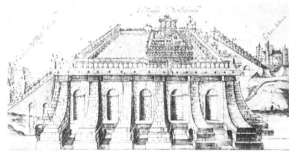

*Aspects of the architectual design of the
Portuguese Synagogue in Amsterdam refer to
the Great Temple of Salomon. The inspiration
must have been fed by the model of the
Temple of Salomon by R. Jacob Juda Leon,
that was exhibited in 1771 in Holland.*

1603, Spanish and Portuguese Jews from Spain arrived at Emden (Germany) in two ships laden with rich cargo and from there were sent to Amsterdam by Rabbi Uri Halevi. On their arrival they rented a house on Joncker Street, opposite the Montelbaans Tower, where after a few weeks Uri Halevi came and circumcised them. This statement is of importance because it indicates that these were Marranos.

It is definitely not true that these Spanish and Portuguese Jews were entirely free to meet openly for worship in Amsterdam at the time. This is not as strange as it may seem if we consider that at that time, in the early 17th century, the Dutch were still in the middle of their Eighty Years War of Liberation against Spain. Also, Amsterdam at the time was a Calvinistic city that had won its particular religious freedom at a high price. This led most

likely to a rather uncompromising stance that loosened as time went on, and the Jews proved themselves to be a valuable addition. However, things first got worse before they got better. The Synod of Dordrecht, concerned about the attraction of Judaism for some Calvinists, even appealed to the States-General to withdraw the freedom of faith. Fortunately, things never got that far. From the marriage registers it may be concluded that most Jews lived in the Vloonburg district, which included the present Waterloo Square, the Korte- en Lange Houtstraat, and the Zwanenburgstraat, the Breedestraat (Jodenbreestraat) and its side streets in the old city. It is certain that after the first arrivals in the city center, the Marranos nearly all settled in the Breestraat and Vloonburg district. The Jews settling in Amsterdam prior to 1620 were nearly all Marranos from Spain and Portugal. Although much remains to be discovered with regard to the early religious services of the Marranos in Amsterdam, it is quite certain that they were not officially permitted in 1620. The first Jewish congregation of Amsterdam, Beth Ja'acob, was formally established in 1604. The second Synagogue was opened by Samuel Palache in 1609. Beth Ya'acob, the elder of the two, opened their own synagogue on the Houtgracht in 1614. Around 1618, after a dispute, members of Beth Ja'acob formed a third congregation, Beth Israel. Uri Ben Joseph Halevi, not a Sephardi himself, was the first Rabbi serving the Jewish community of Amsterdam. The second congregation chose the learned Levantine Joseph Pardo, as their first Sephardi Chief Rabbi. Uri Halevi's Rabbinate was of the utmost importance because he was the first who actually brought the Marranos back to their ancient faith, and thus became the founder of the Jewish community of Amsterdam.

Another prominent figure among the Sephardi was Menasseh ben Israel, known in connection with his visit to England and for his letter to Cromwell. He was the initiator of Hebrew printing in Amsterdam, founded the first Jewish printing house in that city, and published the first Hebrew prayer book in 1627. He died in 1657. He was buried at Beth Haim, the Spanish Portuguese cemetery at Ouderkerk a/d Amstel near Amsterdam. Menasseh ben Israel's fame has spread far beyond the Dutch frontiers. He may be

The ancient Library Ets Haim in the big Portuguese Synagogue in Amsterdam. Pictured are the last two librarians from before 1940: David Montezinos (left) and J. S. da Silva Rosa.

considered one of the most prominent personalities of the 17th century Sephardi community of Amsterdam. He was also a close friend of the great painter Rembrandt van Rhijn, his neighbor on the Breestraat, who contributed four illustrations to Menasseh's book 'La Piedra Gloriosa'.

In 1670, Haham Aboab presented a plan to the Parnassim (the Elders and Wardens of the Synagogue) to build a new Synagogue after the Temple of Solomo in Ionic style in the city. They appointed a committee, which included the members Isaac de Pinto, Samuel Vaz, David Salom de Azevedo, Abraham da Vega, Jacob Aboab Ozorio, Jacob Israel Pereyra and Isaac Henriques Coutino.

Isaac Aboab de Fonseca, first Haham of the new Esnoga, at the age of 80.

The first foundation stone was laid by David van Isaac de Pinto, the second by Mozes Curiel alias Geronimo Nunes da Costa, the third by Joseph Israel Nunes alias Antonio Alvares, the fourth stone by Immanuel de Pinto. The new 'Esnoga' was opened and the first service conducted in 1675. The date 1672 (5432) is specifically mentioned in the text from Psalm V 8, over the main entrance of the Esnoga, in the Jonas Daniel Mèyer square. We must mention the unique Jewish library 'Ets Haim' (Tree of Life), which is housed in one of the low buildings surrounding the Esnoga. This Bibliotheca Sephardica comprises more than 20,000 volumes of printed books and manuscripts, including many which are extremely rare and valuable. It also includes the private library of David Montezinos.

Lifestyle
The Sephardi Jews formed a close-knit community living together in the old center of Amsterdam. They only numbered 1,000 by the year 1700, but were nevertheless the largest

Jewish wedding.

Self-portrait of Rembrandt van Rijn (1606-1669).

Jewish community in Western Europe. They had a network of trust and confidence of kinship and affinity with other Jewish bankers and merchants in the various countries of the Sephardi diaspora (countries around the Mediterrean, Portugal etc). Most of the time these were family ties.

They lived freely in the Amsterdam society and yet they maintained their own traditions and kept their Jewish sanctuary intact. These two elements, Jewish life and Jewish thought, were represented in the artistic imagination of the great painter Rembrandt van Rhijn (1606-1669). It was here that Rembrandt found Jewish neighbors who would model for the masterpieces he painted on Biblical themes (among others the famous 'Jewish

Some Jews reached peaks of wealth in Holland, such as can be witnessed by the Court of Belmonte.

41

Bride'). Whether consciously or by intuition, he seemed to have understood that both the Jews and the Jewish legacy were a part of the common heritage of the Western civilization. One of the best depictions of Jewish life in

'Jews on the street', sketch by Rembrandt, and below it
'Rabbi', painting by Rembrandt.

View of the Jodenbreestraat where the first Marranos from Amsterdam lived.

Amsterdam was painted around 1680 by Emanuel de Witte (1617-1692) and shows the interior of the Spanish-Portuguese Synagogue. In Amsterdam, Jews no longer had to be Marranos. Here they could practice their faith proudly and openly. Something of that pride is reflected in the dimensions, the structure and the beauty of their Synagogues. In their prayers, they adopted the rituals of the Sephardim. In Amsterdam, they were joined by Jews who came from the other great stream of Jewish tradition and rituals; Jews who came from Poland and Lithuania in order to escape the poverty and violence of Eastern Europe in the 16th and 17th centuries. The differences between **Sephardi** and these **Ashkenazi** Jews are too varied to be treated here, but let it suffice to state that they belong more to outer form than inner substance.

In the context of their intellectual history in the 17th century, we come across one of the most important European philosophers,

Baruch Spinoza
Benedict (Baruch) Spinoza was a Dutch philosopher of a Portuguese Marrano family that had escaped to Amsterdam. He had a Jewish education and a good knowledge of medieval Jewish philosophy. His religious views were regarded as heretical by the Sephardi community, which excommunicated him in 1656 under pressure of the Calvinist magistrates of Amsterdam. In 1660, he left Amsterdam. His Theologico-Political Treatise expanded his political philosophy and was the forerunner of biblical higher criticism. His Ethics proved one of the most influential works of western European thought; it is a metaphysics of pantheism, applying Euclidean methods to demonstrate his metaphysical concept of the universe, with ethical corollaries.

Sephardim and Ashkenazim
Of the approximately 15 million Jews who at present exist, nearly 13 million are 'Ashkenazim' compared to a little more than a million Sephardim. Thus, the Judeo-Spaniards comprise barely 10 per cent of the total Jewish population of today. Since the 16th century, however, the cultural predominance of the Sephardim was clear and unquestionable, although

Baruch Spinoza (1632-1677), a Jew of Amsterdam. He was excluded and excommunicated in 1656 from the Jewish community because of what was believed to be his revolt against Jewish orthodoxy. He then earned his living as a lens grinder. Spinoza was not a non-religious Jew, still less an anti-religious Jew. Historians of philosophy have even called him a 'god-intoxicated man'. He believed that scientists and philosophers should be free to pursue their inquiries and speculations about nature wherever their conclusions led them, without any rigid prior commitment to religious dogma. His mathematical precision was in tune with the rationalism of Descartes and Newton. Spinoza is not buried at Beth Haim in Ouderkerk but in the churchyard of the New Church at The Hague. His parents are buried in Ouderkerk and his sister at Beth Haim on the Island of Curaçao.

Historic events

Dutch Jews had a hand in two important developments: the first was the landing at New Amsterdam (New York) in 1654 of not quite two dozen Sephardi; the first Jewish settlers on the North American mainland and the pioneers of what would in time become the world's largest and most prosperous Jewish community. This Jewish settlement in the New Netherland was part of a larger dispersion that saw Dutch Jews trade and settle in coastal Brazil (until they were ousted by the Portuguese), the Island of Curaçao and various oriental outposts. These events will be discussed later. The second development was the return of their brothers to England, from which all Jews had been expelled in 1290. In 1655, the Dutch Jewish leader Menasseh ben Israel (1604-1657) addressed his famous petition to the Lord Protector, the Puritan Oliver Cromwell (1599-1658). Menasseh, whose face is

Commemoration coin with Oliver Cromwell and Menasseh ben Israel.

they were, so to speak, outnumbered. They were superior because of their culture, their liveliness, their genius, their intelligence and even because of their physical endowment and gentlemanly manners.

'Ashkenaz' means 'Germany' in Hebrew. The term 'Germania' appears in old rabbinical literature. In the Jewish book 'Yosipon' of the 10th century, it is used in a more modern sense, and Germany is called 'Eretz Ashkenaz'. Thus the word 'Ashkenazim' is used to designate the Jews from Germany, Central Europe, Poland, Russia, Northern France and includes most of those who live in America. Until the 18th century the Sephardim formed the majority of the Jewish people, but their number declined because of forced baptizing, assimilation, and, of course, the holocaust that wiped out the Sephardi communities of Amsterdam, Hamburg, much of France and Antwerp. Anthropologically it might be said that the Sephardim approximate to the Latins, and owing to the fact of their living separated from other peoples, they have maintained a homogeneous type distinguished by their black or dark brown hair, oval face, elongated, narrow skull with sloping forehead; an appearance in short, that is Eastern and Mediterranean. The Ashkenazi Jews is more West-European, less Oriental. Many of them have fair or red hair, round head and face and are short of stature. They pronounce Hebrew with the accent of North Palestine and their language is 'Yiddish', a mixture of the original Hebrew with the Slavonic tongues and medieval German spoken in the ghettos.

The Jewish group that did not go to Spain followed another road. Also fleeing from the Babylonians, and after fighting in Mesopotamia, where they were beaten, they made for the North of Europe. They came from the tribe of Askenaz. According to Genesis, Ashkenaz was the son of

43

immortalized in an etching by Rembrandt, came to England in 1655 and remained there for two years. Menasseh's petition was not formally granted, but from 1656 onward, Jews were allowed to settle in England and establish their synagogues. In the nineteenth and twentieth centuries, English Jews would play a central part in the resettlement of Palestine and the rebirth of Zionism.

Gomer, a descendant of Noah and of Japhet, which indicates a people of the Indogermanic group in the genealogical tables. In the Bible, the word refers rather to a region of the Armenian highlands than to a people. Assyrian inscriptions of the 7th century refer to the 'Ash-ku-sa', allies of Assyria and probably identical with the Scythians. Flavius Josephus identifies Ashkenaz with the city of Rhagae, in the center of Media, while the rabbinical tradition indicates a territory between Kurdistan and Armenia, and later 'Targum' the Roman province of Asia. Scattered about the world after the Diaspora, the leaders of both branches realized that it was necessary for them to unify rites, political activities, taxes, judges and courts. But the Sephardim, who thought themselves superior, who were truly orthodox, and kept scrupulously to the letter of the Talmud and did not wish to obey the dictates of the Ashkenazi rabbis. Thus the 'differential fact' originated, with all its consequences. Three tendencies existed within Judaism in those days: the Babylonian, symbolized by Rabbi Alfassi, of the old rabbinical academies; the Spanish personified in Maimonides, and the Germanic of Rashi. The Sephardim attained the predominance of Alfassi and Maimonides. Polygamy was permitted among them, which was a great sin for the Ashkenazim, and they practiced the Levirate, the Mosaic law which obliged the brother of a deceased husband to marry the widow (his sister-in-law), which constituted incest for the Ashkenazim.

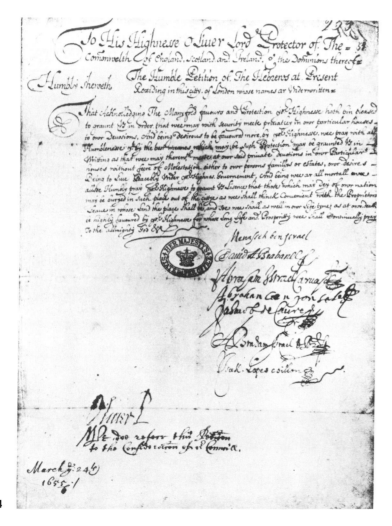

Petition of Menasseh ben Israel to Cromwell.

Speaking Stones

'Because I know, You will kill me
and bring me to the House of
Gathering of everybody who lives'.
(Job, 30:23)

'The very names recorded here are
strange, of foreign accent and of
different climes; Alvares and Rivera
interchange with Abraham and
Jacob of old Times'.
(H. W. Longfellow)

Aerial overview of Ouderkerk a/d Amstel with
Sephardi cemetery Beth Haim (courtesy KLM
Aerocarte).

45

It had been an arduous and long journey for the Jews that had come from Spain and Portugal. But Amsterdam finally provided them with a climate that proved a stimulus for the building of a cohesive community. It had not come easy and restrictions still barred them from certain professions. The establishment then of their own cemetery – although not a smooth affair – can be considered as the acknowledgement of their just and deserved place in Amsterdam society.

Upon entering the gates of the old Jewish cemetery Beth Haim at Ouderkerk a/d Amstel, one wonders about the oddity of giving the resting place such a paradoxical name. For Beth Haim means quite literally House of the Living. It is, however, to be understood as just that, a paradox; an euphenistic way of describing the deceased; a continuous reminder that man may, but the past does not die.

Initial difficulties

The history of the cemetery Beth Haim is connected with the establishement and development of the Portuguese community in Amsterdam. Although the Portuguese Jews were allowed and did settle in several cities – in 1604, the Portuguese Jews were offered complete equality with the inhabitants of Alkmaar – most of them settled in Amsterdam. With the arrival of small groups of refugees, two, later three, communities were formed in succession. These were Marranos from Portugal and from Spain who reverted to Judaism.

The adjustment was not always easy for the new immigrants. Amongst themselves, the Portuguese spoke the Portuguese language or Castellano. In official documents, for political reasons, they were referred to as belonging to the Portuguese Nation, though they were for the most part of Spanish origin. The communal records were kept in Portuguese. Spanish was used only occasionally for the translations of the Bible, Psalms and other writings. Accordingly, most of the gravestones bear inscriptions in Portuguese and/or Hebrew, at least until the end of the eighteenth century.

Right after the first settlement, the Jews attempted to obtain permission to buy a plot of land to bury their dead. It proved a difficult matter for the magistrate of Amsterdam was unwilling to grant permission. In 1602, the Jews succeeded, however, in purchasing land near Groet, a town in the vicinity of Alkmaar. In 1606 and 1608, the burgomasters of Amsterdam again refused permission. Consequently, they continued to be dependent on the Groet cemetery. The transportation of the deceased over such a long distance naturally produced serious difficulties, not in the least because of the tolls which had to be paid when churches were passed.

In Amsterdam, meanwhile, three communities had been formed. The first was called Beth Jacob -'House of Jacob'-, the second (founded in 1608) Newhe Shalom -'Abode of Peace'- and the third, Beth Israel. In 1609, shortly after the foundation of Beth-Jacob, that community established a society called Bikkur Holim – 'Visiting the Sick' – which had as its objective not only to provide for the needy sick but also to wash the dead – to accompany the mourners at the funeral and to prepare the first meal afterwards.

In 1639, the society Gemiluth Hasadim – 'Performance of Pious Deeds' – was set up. It occupied itself with acts of charity for the dying and the deceased. Under the supervision of this brotherhood, the subdivisions Avodath ha-Qodesh – 'Holy Service' – (to carry the dead from the deceased's house to the boat), and Mishmereth ha-Bayith – 'Service of the House' – (to place the dead on the bier) were established. It was the brotherhood Bikkur Holim for which the journey to Groet became too heavy a financial burden.

In 1614, the three communities were finally able to buy a piece of land in Ouderkerk for the sum of 2,700 florins from Jacob Backer, a justice of Amsterdam. The purchase deed was signed by Francisco, alias Ishac, Franco Medeyros, one of the founders of Neweh Shalom. Both communities had appointed delegates in whose names the final purchase deed was to be drafted. They were Dr. Simon Lopes Rosa, alias Dr. Abraham the elder, and Francisco Mendes Trancoso, alias Jacob Franco. On June 2, 1614, the signing by the delegates took place in presence of the parnassim (governors) of the two communities and Isaac Franco Medeyros. The tomb of this Isaac in the shape of a pagoda is to be found in the oldest part of the cemetery.

In this same year, the first burial took place: the child Joseph Senior, son of a parnas. The small gravestone bears the inscription of a Hebrew poem in which the child himself speaks and says that he is the first to be buried on the Beth Haim. At first, the funeral met some opposition from the local population and Isaac Franco Medeyros was sent to The Hague to complain. The States of Holland ordered the bailiff of Amstelland to see to it that the funerals could take place without disturbance. The funerals, however, were to take place

without ceremony and unobtrusively. After the land had been adapted for use as a cemetery, it was officially put into use in 5376/1616. This date is found on the sign above the former landing stage where a gate probably formed part of a fence along the Bullewijk. Yet difficulties remained throughout 1618 and 1621. In 1621, the bailiff had to order the gates along the Amsteldijk to be opened for the funeral processions of the

The transportation of the deceased.

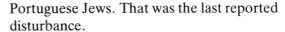

In the painting by Van Ruysdael, the ruins of the castle of Egbert van Aemstel still dominate the location of what is to become Beth Haim.

Portuguese Jews. That was the last reported disturbance.

Remarkable gravestones

At the request of relatives, the remains of those buried in Groet were removed to Ouderkerk after the closing of the former cemetery. The last removal took place in 1634. We know of more purchases of adjacent pieces of land in Ouderkerk (1663, 1671, 1690). In 1923, all the land designated for burial was used. The members of the Portuguese Jewish community, however, were very attached to the Beth Haim in Ouderkerk. It was inconceivable to them to bury a member of the community elsewhere. Therefore, an 18th century part of the cemetery was raised with three meters of sand. Permission to bury without religious objections was acquired in this way. It had been planned that the raised piece of land would be sufficient for another 40 years of burials. It was estimated that in 1963 a similar lack of burial ground would be encountered. Of course the barbaric events during World War II changed that prediction.

This oldest Sephardic cemetery in Europe, where from 1614 till the 18th century some 8,000 Jews were buried is situated along the Amstel river at Ouderkerk. Shaded by trees, silent, and sometimes forgotten, it bears testimony to all the great men of learning and trade that lie buried here. At present Beth Haim is a novelty to visit, and not in the least on account of the remarkable gravestones. David Henriques de Castro wrote in his famous book *'Keur van Grafstenen'* (1883) about Beth Haim: 'A location famous for its historical meanings to the native country, witnessing greatness and humility. Here stood the first castle of the Nobility of Aemstel, built under the authority of Egbert van Aemstel in the midst of the 12th century, that had been destroyed by the Kennemers under Gijsbrecht II in 1204, and was thus destined to be the last resting place for the exiles, who, at the Pyrenees once saw their sun go down and came to Amsterdam in order to be free to profess their religion again and to live their life in peace and freedom till the end.'
'Thou shalt not make unto thee any graven image, or any likeness...' This biblical prohibition has always ruled the burial

traditions of the Jews. One will find, therefore, as a rule no statues, no images of any kind, and certainly no depictions of God or of biblical scenes, on their tombstones. A carefully observed inhibition is usually apparant. The stones of Beth Haim make an extraordinary exception to that stern rule. Instead of displaying the usual sober appearance, one can witness at Beth Haim a bewildering collection of sometimes even abundantly sculpted tombstones. A visitor to Beth Haim, lost in his reflections, will hear the stones speaking to him. They speak of the Sephardi community of Amsterdam.

Workmanship and execution
The diversity of the stones represent the 'melting-pot character' of the Amsterdam Jewish community at the time. Some of the buried here were orthodox Jews, some families had lived as Catholics for two centuries and had become estranged from the Jewish faith, while others can be characterized as humanists with a Jewish background! From

Oriental influence can be seen in the four tombs of the de Mercado family and that of Rachel Jessurun Brandao.

an art history point of view, the tombstones are very interesting because of the workmanship and execution.

Many Dutch sculptors, finding no work in Catholic communities after the Iconoclasm (1567), were in great demand to sculpture the Jewish tombstones. This is particularly interesting since the sculpturing of tombstones is predominantly a Catholic and not a Jewish tradition. Perhaps these converted Jews that lie buried here were outwardly Christian but adhered inwardly to the Jewish faith. Unfortunately, only a few tombstones of all the people buried here are still visible.

Differences, though, in wealth, status and occupations are still evident. The stones of the scholars Menasseh Ben Israel and Joseph Athias for example, have only simple inscriptions while richly ornamented stones are typical of the wealthy De Mercado family. The depiction of God before Samuel in the Temple on one stone is a very Christian presentation. Derived from the Renaissance culture are the fashionable 'memento mori'-emblems (skulls, little angels or putto's, hourglass). They are a reminder to the living that they too will die. It is quite possible that the pictures on these stones were chosen by the sculptors themselves. They were more than likely all Christians since Jews could not become members of the Guilds. Nevertheless, the choice of the subjects clearly suggests a Jewish influence. A good example in this respect is the beautiful stone of Mozes of Mordechai Senior (5490/1730). The stone expresses the fundaments of Jewish religion in eleven scenes, among them Mordechai entering the city. No Christian could have made such a choice! Attention should also be

Grave of Eliahu Montalto (1616) who was a Marrano from Portugal. Montalto went on to become the personal physician of the Duke of Tuscany. Later, he became the physician of Maria de Medici, wife of Henry IV of France.

Tombstone of Mozes van Mordechai Senior (1730).

drawn to The House of the Seven Rounds (the Rodeamento house, or house of purification). In the depiction on the stone from 1705, the ritual washing takes place during which seven circular rounds were made around the bier of the deceased.

Known and unknown
The number of physicians buried here is exceptionally large, and includes the graves of:
Dr. Eliahu Montalto, the personal physician of Maria de Medici and of the Duke of Tuscany;
Dr. Joseph Buenos, who was called to the death-bed of the Prince Maurits;
Dr. Efraim Bueno; whose son was painted by Rembrandt;
Dr. Benjamin Musaphia, the personal physician of King Christian of Denmark;
Menasseh Ben Israel, a Rabbi and scientist;
The Parents of Spinoza.
Dr. Isaac Orobria de Castro, a strong opponent of Spinoza;
The Teixeiras family, bankers;
The Machados;
The Pintos;
Dr. Sarphati;
Jozef Mendes da Costa, sculptor.

Efraim Bueno, physician; an etching by Rembrandt.

All the Marranos, all their descendants; and all the Portuguese Jews of Amsterdam are buried here in Ouderkerk. There are 27,000 graves in the oldest part of the cemetery. In this oldest part of the cemetery is located the very first stone, the tombstone of a child. The small stone comprises a Hebrew inscription with a deeply emotional content. *'On this place I have turned over under the dust. Shortly after my birth I left the world. With me the Beth Haim has been consecrated. In the year 5374 I have left for Eden. Joseph was the name that they gave me. I was the son of David Senior, his name being my pride. In this grave I have been laid down on the second of Ijar 5374 (April 11, 1614)'.*

Tombstone of Joseph de David Senior. Joseph, soon after birth, was the first to be buried at Beth Haim in 1614.

The father of Baruch de Spinoza, Michael de Espinoza, was buried at Beth Haim in 1654.

Samuel Senior Teixeira (1716) and his wife Rachel Teixeira de Mattos (1717). In reference to his name, the stone depicts the image of Samuel in the Temple (I Samuel 3). The stone also portrays Rachel, wife of the patriarch Jacob, dying at the time of Benjamin's birth, as related in Genesis 35:17.

Esther de la Penha-Gabay Henriques (1697). Her stone shows commercial ships approaching their house along the Boompjes in Rotterdam.

Ysak Franco Medeyros (1623) made the purchase of the land for the cemetery. The pagoda shape of this tomb is noteworthy. (Opposite page)

David da Rocha (1708). The picture of King David at the top of his stone not only refers to his first name but also to his musical abilities.

David de Daniel de la Penha (1750). A marble gravestone executed in rococo style with the family coat of arms with the marquess' coronet.

*Abraham Zagache (1685) and his wife Sara
(1670). Two beautifully sculptured tombstones
in baroque style.*

Abraham de Chaves (1730).

David Raphael de Meza (1716). The inscription above the table with the twelve shew-breads reads: 'This is the table that is before the Lord' (ezekiel 41:22).

Economic Factors

As can be grasped from the chapter about 'The Low Countries', the initial establishment of the Dutch Sephardi community in Amsterdam (1595-1608) coincided in the main with the economic warfare between the Spanish Crown and the newly independant northern provinces of Holland. After the division of the original 17 provinces into a Spanish dominated southern part and a free Calvinistic northern part a stalemate had been reached and mutual hostilities were played out in the market place rather than the battle field. Until 1595, most of the trade involving Portuguese East India spices and Brazilian sugar to northern Europe was in the hands of Marranos residing in Antwerp. This did not only change due to persecution of these Jews in Antwerp, but certainly also by the general maritime blockade of the southern provinces by the States-General in the north. This obviously stimulated the role that the Sephardi community in Amsterdam was soon going to play. The

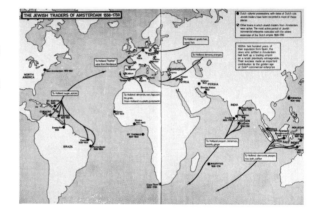

maritime ban likewise animated the rise and/or founding of other Sephardi communities at Hamburg, Altona (both Germany), Rotterdam and Rouen and Nantes (the latter two in France).

The first Portuguese and Jewish merchants of Amsterdam more or less took over from the Antwerp exporters of colonial wares from Portugal. The embargoes of traffic on the river

A general view of the hussle and bussle of Amsterdam during the peak of its powers.

Scheldt and the reciprocal ban of river traffic between the North and the South Netherlands were lifted in the summer of 1608. The subsequent Twelve Years Truce lasted till April, 1621. This 12-year interval proved to be one of the most vigorous and dramatic growth periods for the Sephardi community in Amsterdam in particular, and for the North Netherlands in general. Dutch Sephardi Jews signed in this period a vast majority of the freight contracts for voyages to and from Portugal. A significant number of voyages, though, were contracted for Marocco and Spain. An outstanding Dutch Jew in the salt trade at this time was Bento Osorio, who was in fact the richest Jew in Holland before 1640.

New trades

During the Twelve Years Truce the Dutch traffic to Guinea developed rapidly; and, again, the Sephardi merchants played a leading role. The volume of Dutch trade with equatorial West Africa grew from about 20 to 40 ships annually. Vessels chartered by Amsterdam Jews reportedly fetched slaves from West Africa to bring them directly to Brazil and the Spanish Caribbean. By 1620, Dutch Sephardi Jews numbered approximately 1,200 of whom at least 1,000 resided in Amsterdam. The chief obstacle, however, to further growth of this community was exclusion from the guilds, organizations that governed the traditional trades and crafts. Jews were practically everywhere forbidden from becoming storekeepers or from practicing crafts. They were allowed to enter guilds that governed the practice of medicine, pharmacies and book retail. It was, actually, the emergence of entirely new trades and

Dutch Sephardi Jews signed a vast majority of the freight contracts for voyages to and from Portugal, Marocco and Spain.

Being excluded from traditional trades and crafts, the Sephardi Jews set out to introduce entirely new trades such as printing. Shown here is the title page of Menasseh ben Israel's book 'La Piedra Gloriosa', which was printed in Menasseh's Hebrew printing house.

industries that sprang from the burgeoning colonial trade and for which no previously established guild structure existed.

These phenomena were largely responsible for the rise of the relatively numerous Jewish artisans. Diamond cutting and polishing, for instance, was not only new to Amsterdam, but also to the Jews who began practicing it. Several other of these Jewish' crafts were tobacco-molling, silk-weaving, sugar-refining, chocolate-making and, last but not least, printing. Book production especially took off on a large scale.

Yet this time of prosperity was interfered with by the expiration of the Twelve Years Truce in 1621. For two decades, Dutch shipping and cargoes were again officially excluded from Spain, Portugal, the Flemish ports and southern Italy by decree of the Spanish monarch, Philip IV. The Sephardi Jews of

Amsterdam and Rotterdam were unquestionably the foremost victims of these embargoes for they had specialized above all in trade with

Portugal. A sizeable part of the Dutch Sephardi community migrated, for the most part to Hamburg and Glückstadt. Lack of alternatives forced the remaining Sephardi community in Amsterdam – that was barely if at all capable with dealing for the unemployed and poor – to persist in trading with Portugal in spite of massive obstacles. They switched from Dutch ships to Hanseatic, French and English vessels, and made use of neutral ports to be able to show that the cargoes contained nothing of Dutch origin and had not been loaded on Dutch soil. Needless to say, the Sephardi merchants suffered losses, some spectacularly so.

West India Company

Reflecting the Spanish and Portuguese enterprises before them, the Dutch had become more and more interested in colonial affairs. However, they were in no position to install more than just small settlements and to establish a few naval posts along the route of their spice trades. Created in 1602, the Dutch East India Company, supported by the Dutch war fleet, backed by the home government and well provided with financial resources, was particularly active in Indonesia. It brought fabulous profits which in time made Amsterdam the financial capital of the world.

Faced with the end of the Twelve Years Truce in 1621, and the resulting recession in Holland, the Dutch next founded the West India Company. It was to become the strong-arm of the Dutch merchants who had their mind set on the Portuguese spice islands and Brazil. The singular Dutch interest in the aims of The West India Company is best expressed in the ineffective pleads by Dutch Sephardi Jews to

King Philip IV of Spain.

Warehouse and dock of the East India Company on the Oostenburg, Amsterdam, 1694.

the government to secure official immunity from confiscation by the West India Company of sugar transported from Brazil to Portugal in Portuguese vessels on their behalf.

The West India Company's subjugation of north-east Brazil in 1630, however, changed things considerably, not in the least for the Dutch Sephardi Jews. These and other events will be discussed in the next chapter.

Adventures in South America and the Caribbean

As early as 1572, Dutch ships appeared before the coast of Panama. At the end of the 16th century, there was a regular trade with the Caribbean area. The Dutch exchanged or bought dyewood, tobacco and sugar. The most important article, however, was salt for which there was a large demand. Previously salt came from France, Spain and Portugal, and from the islands in the Atlantic Ocean.

The ban by the Spanish king on the export of salt to the Netherlands was a big mistake, because there were plenty of saltpans (salinas), not controlled by the Spanish. Moreover, there were very large saltpans at Punta de Araya, a cape on the north coast of South America (presently Venezuela) that were not under Spanish control. The coast between the delta of the Orinoco River and that of the Amazon River (the 'wild coast')

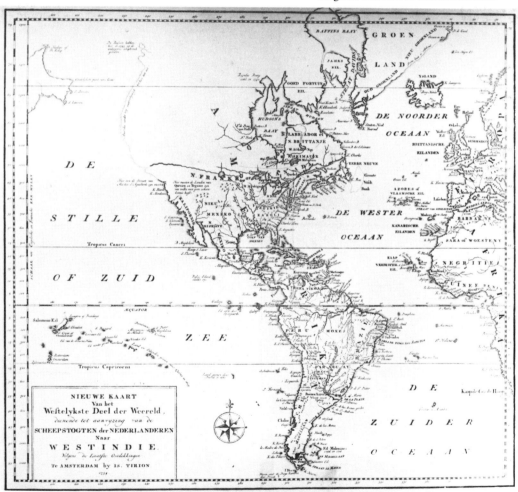

A map showing the journeys of Dutch ships to the West Indies, and left from it Frigates en route to South America.

62

had been frequented by Dutch ships since the first part of the 17th century. Merchants from Zeeland in the south-west of the Netherlands were especially active in the trade on the 'wild coast'. Since 1616, Jan de Moor and the Courten brothers had settlements on Essequibo (nowadays French Guayana). As we have seen, the early 16th century witnessed Dutch traders on the Brazilian coast. The period immediately preceding the Twelve Years Truce saw a busy trade with Portugal (the Portuguese being very prominent in Brazil) since South America was off limits for all but Spanish ships. This increased significantly during the Twelve Years Truce. Dutch merchants' ships sometimes even sailed under Portuguese flag to carry the products from Brazil. With the advent of the end of the Twelve Years Truce, the Dutch (Sephardi) merchants saw themselves confronted with a particular problem. How to continue their profitable trade? As early as 1591, a Dutch

merchant, **Willem Usselincx**, who had come to Middelburg from Antwerp, had suggested the concept of a major trading company for the Americas. His appeal had met at the time with little enthusiasm. Now, however, Usselincx' vision became an appealing one. Yet, although Usselincx had envisioned his trading company to be a tool to combat the Spaniards, he was not in favor of a semi-military company such as many others were advocating. Usselincx was not alone in his reservations. Some merchants feared that drastic actions could lead to the resumption of embargoes that would intefere with their lucrative trade. Still the voices of force prevailed. When in 1621 the Twelve Years Truce came to an end, the **West India Company** (WIC) was set up. Instead of the trading company Usselincx had proposed, however, it became a roving privateer company.

The board of the WIC was managed by five chambers: Amsterdam, Zeeland, Maze (Rotterdam, Delft, Dordrecht), the Quarter of the North (Alkmaar, Hoorn, Enkhuizen, Edam, Medemblik and Monnikendam), Friesland and Groningen (Stad en Lande). Whenever deemed necessary, they could call a general meeting. These meetings of the nineteen gentlemen ('De Heren Negentien') were held alternately in Amsterdam and Middelburg. During the first six years Amsterdam was the hostess, and Middelburg the following two years. Amsterdam held a domineering position as she produced three of the seven million guilders budget. The States-General (the legislative body of the Government) yielded a great influence. On the 12th of July, 1622, the States-General came to an agreement with the West Indian

Willem Usselincx

Usselincx (1567-ca. 1647) was an Antwerp born Dutch merchant. In 1591, he established himself in Amsterdam, where he was an agent for Spanish and Portuguese trading houses. There he vainly tried to establish a major trading firm for the Americas. Not until 1621, at the conclusion of the Twelve Years Truce, was such a company established by the States-General. It was, however, rather different from the one that Usselincx had envisioned. Usselincx had argued to no avail for a limiting of the influence by the excecutive board of the WIC favoring the shareholders. Also, he advocated that the soon to be conquered territories be populated by Protestants from Holland. In 1643, Usselincx became an agent for Sweden in the Netherlands. He made propaganda for colonization of new territories, and came into conflict with the States of Holland on account of his criticism of its policies. Usselincx died in poverty.

West India Company

The very first suggestion, that in due time led to the establishment of the West India Company (WIC), came from Willem Usselincx in the 1590s. He saw such a company as a means to colonize areas in the Americas and combat the Spaniards. In 1621, the States-General gave the charter to the newly WIC for the west coast of Africa, America, all islands of the Pacific and the east coast of New Guinea. Contrary to the East India Company, the WIC received no sovereignty rights; in order to wage actual war it needed the explicit approval of the States-General of Holland. The WIC was in name an incorporated trading company, however, in reality it was little more than a roving privateer company. The capture of a Spanish silver fleet by one of the WIC's commanders, Piet Hein, is both a good example of these practices as well as an event still celebrated in Dutch history. The WIC gained areas in Brazil, Africa, West Indies (the islands Aruba, Bonaire, Curaçao, Essequibo, Demerary, Berbice, St. Eustachias, Saba

The so-called West India house of the West India Company at Amsterdam, built in 1641. **63**

Company, deciding to outfit a fleet, known as the 'Nassau Fleet'. This fleet reached the West Indies by way of Mexico. In 1630, the Dutch conquered Olinda and Recife in the district of Pernambuco (on the east coast of Brazil) from the Portuguese and in 1636, the Dutch prince Johan Maurits, Count of Nassau – Siegen was appointed as Governor of this new colony. The foothold that was thus gained on the Brazilian coast was further fortified by the construction of two fortresses, 'Nassau' and 'Oranje'. In due time these strongholds were lost to the Portuguese (1654).

3

NIEUWE IN-TEYCKENINGE
ENDE
Verhooginge der Capitalen vande Ge-octroyeerde West-Indische
COMPAGNIE.

Lʃoo de Hoogh:ende Mog:Heeren Staten Generael der Ver-eenighde Nederlanden, by hare Reʃolutie van den 19 Iunij 1636, geauthoriʃeert ende machtigh ghemaeckt hebben de Vergaderinge der Negenthiene, ende de Reʃpective Cameren der ʃelver Compagnie, om op nieuws te mogen open ʃtellen ende te ontfangen vande t'ʃamentlijcke Participanten de verhooginge van hare Capitalen voor een derde Part; dewelcke van ʃoodanige kracht, recht ende nature ʃullen weʃen, in bate ende voordeele jegenwoordigh by de ghemelte Compagnie weʃende, ofte hier na maels te verkrygen, ghelijck als ofte die van aenbegin ingebrocht ende geteyckent waren geweeʃt : dat oock de ʃelve Participanten vry ʃal ʃtaen op haer behagen, de voornoemde verhooginge in ʃoodanige Camer ofte Cameren te doen als ʃy ʃullen goet vinden, niet tegenʃtaende hunne origenele teyckeninghen, ofte daer ʃy Actie verkreghen hebben, in een andere Kamere gedaen waren. SO OIST, dat by deʃen alle ende een yeder, die het ʃoude moghen aen gaen, wert ghenotificeert, dat de Bewinthebberen in hare reʃpective Kameren vanden eerʃten Auguʃti tot den eerʃten October naeʃtkomende gereet ʃullen weʃen t'ontfangen ʃoodanige inteyckeninghe ende verhooginghe als de Participanten, ofte die haer Actie hebben, ʃullen willen doen : waer toe de Gedeputeerde Bewinthebberen ʃit-dagh ʃullen houden alle werck-daghen, van 's morgens ten negen uren tot elf uren. Welcke ingeteyckende gelden ende verhooghde Capitalen opgebracht ende betaelt ʃullen worden in dry termynen; waer van de eerʃte ʃal verʃchijnen den eerʃten November naeʃtkomende: de tweede op den eerʃten Martij 1637, ende de derde ofte laetʃte op den eerʃten Iulij daer aen volgende. Des ʃo yemant van ʃin mocht weʃen alle zyne verhooginghe ghereet ende in een reyʃe te betalen, daer voren ʃal ghenieten het Rabat teghen acht ten hondert in 't Iaer, pro rato vanden tijt.

D'Een ʃegget d'ander voort.

25. Bekendmaking van een nieuwe emiʃʃie van aandelen van de WIC uit 1636.

57

7

4

1

2

5

6

1 The ship of Prince Johan Maurits.

2 The capture of a Spanish fleet loaded with silver (hence the name 'silver fleet') by WIC commander Piet Heyn is an event still celebrated in Dutch folklore.

3 In 1636, Prince Johan Maurits, Count of Nassau-Siegen, was appointed as Governor of the newly conquered territories in Brazil.

4 After establishing themselves in Brazil, the Dutch West India Company set about minting temporary money.

5 In 1632, the fortress 'Oranje' was built on the Brazilian coast.

6 A floormap of the fortress 'Maurits', built in 1637, aimed to protect the Dutch settlement on the Brazilian coast.

7 A document of the West India Company announcing the issue of shares.

Gains and losses

The conclusion of the Twelve Years Truce – a period during which the Amsterdam Sephardi Jews had prospered so much – brought renewed embargoes by the Spanish King, Philip IV, and thus hardship to their community. As a matter of fact, this situation lasted for about 20 years, right up to the secession of Portugal from Spain in 1640.

The subjugation by the West India Company of north-east Brazil brought about a definitive turn of events for the Sephardi merchants. The fighting caused some considerable damage to the sugar plantations of the conquered Pernambuco region, but production began to recover in the late 1630s. It stimulated a thriving, if temporary, direct traffic between Brazil and Holland. This business was handled by private merchants paying fees and tolls to the WIC. From the start, Dutch Sephardi Jews played an important role in this trade. Making use of their former contacts, they carried on where they left off before, be it that they now acted under the aegis of the WIC. Naturally, their pre-eminence can be explained by their long experience in the Brazil trade and their fluency in both Dutch and Portuguese.

During the period that the Pernambuco region was under control of the WIC (1630-1654), Sephardi Jews settled there, too. Although most were Dutch Jews, some were former local New Christians that had reverted to Judaism. Together they totalled 1,450, or roughly one third of the white population in the territory, including the Portuguese Catholic planters.

The WIC's gains in Brazil, while they lasted, did much to strengthen the Dutch Sephardi community in Amsterdam after the recession

caused by the expiration of the Twelve Years Treaty. It did, however, very little for the diversification of their commercial base. There was a growth in tobacco production, possibly under influence of the new Brazil trade. During the 1641-1648 period, with Portugal trying to assert its independence from Spain and King Joao IV in dire need of arms and ammunition, the Sephardi Jews became active in the arms trade.

The year 1654 saw the **collapse of Netherlands Brazil**. The loss of the forts 'Nassau' and 'Oranje' and with it Dutch influence meant an abrupt end to the flourishing Sephardi community there. This setback for both the

and St. Martin) and North America (New Netherland). The trade became increasingly focused on the slave trade, a remarkable fact given the rather strict religious persuasions of its members. The WIC engaged in no actual colonizations that required the bringing over of Dutch residents, since its shareholders were more interested in short term gains than the making of investments that would yield profits in the long run. This was made particularly evident in the short-lived settlements in Brazil. With the conclusion of the war with Spain, the privateering on Spanish ships had to end. As a result, the financial position of the WIC was considerably weakened. In 1674, it was liquidated. In 1675, a second WIC was established. It was to be solely a trading firm with as its main activity the slave trade. Curaçao became the major depot for this trade. The WIC engaged also in the export of sugar from Surinam. The fourth English War (1780-1784) brought the second WIC to its demise. Its possessions and debts were taken over by the States-General.

Slave market in Mauritsstad, Brazil, around 1640. (Top)

The salt trade with Brazil increased considerably. (Left)

Signatures of Johan Maurits, Diederik van Waerdenburgh, Sigimund van Schoppe, Hendrik Cornelisz. Loncq, Chrestofle Arciszwsky, Piet Heyn, Jan Cornelisz. Lichthart and João Vieira. (Far left)

Collapse

Events had slowly changed for the worse in the Pernambuco district of Dutch Brazil. On April 18, 1642 Count Johan Maurits, under whom the forts 'Nassau' and 'Oranje' were erected, had been called back to Holland. During his absence, a popular revolt

Jewish community in the Pernambuco region as well as for the one in the homeland – the communities kept close ties with the smaller one in Brazil always acknowledging the pre-eminence of the one in Amsterdam – was more than compensated for by the sudden breakthrough in Spanish trade that materialized at the time. A complex set of undercurrents played a role in this somewhat surprising change of Spanish attitude. There was, of course, the Treaty of Münster (1648) that re-opened Dutch-Spanish relations. Under its provisions, Jewish subjects of the Netherlands were reluctantly permitted to trade with Spain, through either Catholic or Protestant correspondents. The resurgence of vehement Inquisition pressure on the Portuguese New Christians in Castile, and the bankruptcy of the Spanish State, caused many prominent merchants and bankers to leave both Castile and the Spanish Netherlands. The Sephardi communities in Amsterdam, Rotterdam and Hamburg saw an influx of wealth from these Portuguese New Christians. One such Jew was De Pinto, an active businessman from Lisbon and, later, Antwerp, who established himself in Rotterdam. He soon became a leader of the community there. He also invested heavily in the East and West India Companies as many of the new and wealthy arrivals did, acquiring with it a stake and thereby interest in the exploits of the WIC. This by itself explains the intertwining of the Sephardi Jews with the fate of the WIC, and their settling in the Caribbean. The newcomers brought besides capital and esteem active business connections with Spain. These families – who often reverted to Judaism upon reaching the Netherlands – were among the dozen or so richest Jews in Holland, and were to dominate Dutch Sephardi community life and politics for a long time. Accompanying the collapse of the WIC's holdings on the Brazilian coast was the gradual decline of trade with Portugal. Most significant of all in reducing the importance of Dutch Jewish dealings with Portugal was the sudden vigorous upsurge of sugar imports into Europe from various parts of the Caribbean, notably Cuba, Martinique and Barbados. This process, which began in the late 1640s, culminated in the devastation of the plantations of Netherlands Brazil by the Portuguese insurgents in that territory. The Sephardi communities in Amsterdam and Hamburg played a role in this too. For it was they, who orchestrated much of the import of sugar from the Caribbean Islands which had fallen to the WIC. The European market was flooded with against the Dutch provincial goverment broke out. High income taxes levied by the Dutch, toll money and religious contrasts were the cause of the uprising. Also, the Portuguese, who had after all established themselves originally in Pernambuco, were worried about the penetration by foreign powers in the basin of the Amazon River. Expelling the French from Maranhao, they settled in the districts of Ceara, Maranhao and Para. From there they waged war on the Dutch, and supported the Portuguese planters who had risen before. The popular revolt against the WIC is still one of the highpoints in the history of Brazil. The Portuguese had planned to take all prominent Dutch as prisoners after capturing the two forts. The subsequent fight at Monte de Tobacos was won by the Portuguese. They were also successful with the capture of the forts. On the sea, however, they fared less well. The Dutch commander Lichthart defeated the Portuguese fleet. Yet, with the forts 'Nassau' and 'Oranje' gone, the Dutch sorely lacked a good base. In 1647, the masters in Holland decided to equip a fleet with 6,000 soldiers and send it to Brazil in an attempt to reverse matters. This endeavor was unsuccessful. The outbreak of the First English War kept the Dutch warships at home, and consequently hostilities in the Brazil area ceased. In a last attempt, the Dutch States-General sent an envoy to Lisbon to request the Portuguese king to lay aside his territorial claims for the Brazil areas previously occupied by the Dutch. It was to be in vain.

Sugar factory in the Caribbean.

An inscription above the doorway of a house in Amsterdam illustrates the involvement of the Sephardi Jews with the Caribbean trade.

sugar. The result was a collapse in sugar prices on the Amsterdam Exchange. This drastic fall in sugar prices took place in the years 1655-1657, and proved a decisive turning point in the history of Europe's commerce with the New World: prices never again approached their former levels.

The Emergence of Curaçao

In 1654, when the Sephardi were expelled from Brazil many returned to Holland, but some went to the Guyanas (Surinam), Barbados (which was the main center before the rise of Curaçao), Martinique, Jamaica and

New-Amsterdam (later New York). In the Latin-American colonies, that stood under domination of Spain, Portugal and France, the Jews faced the continuous threat of persecution. It was also during the 1650's, that Amsterdam Sephardi Jews established a colony on **Curaçao** which was shortly to become the most important of all the Jewish communities in the New World.
After 1648, Dutch ships venturing to the coast of the Spanish American mainland with slaves, cloth and spices – the three items most in demand with the Spanish colonists – at first

enjoyed only a sporadic success in evading the obstacles set up by the Spanish bureaucracy and garrisons. Regular contact between Curaçao and the neighboring South American mainland began only in or around 1657, setting in motion the shift which was soon to transform Curaçao into the Amsterdam of the Caribbean. The first Jewish settlers cultivated tobacco and sugar cane. Most of them lived around the still present Jewish cemetery of Beth Haim. After 1664, commerce increased. The Jews left their plantations to become

merchants. By 1748, there were 1,500 to 2,000 Jews in Curaçao, half of the total number of white inhabitants.
In 1662, Philip IV of Spain signed the notorious slaving Asiento with some Genoese businessmen, stipulating that slaves to be shipped to the Spanish Indies under this contract were not to be obtained from the Portuguese with whom Spain was still at war. To meet this demand, the Genoese turned to the Dutch West India Company which, in a series of contracts signed in Amsterdam, agreed to act as an individual licensing agency.

The Jewish community in Brazil (Nassau)

Many Portuguese Jews found their new fatherland in Brazil where they enjoyed religious freedom. During the Dutch occupation many Jews from Amsterdam arrived. They went into the sugar trade and financing of sugar mills. Some of them, such as Duarte Saraiva, Jacob Dessine, Fernand de Vale and Moises Navarro, had sugar mills of their own. They spoke Dutch and Portuguese and had many contacts in Amsterdam. Rabbi Isaac Aboabda Fonseca from Amsterdam, was working in Pernambuco. The famous Rabbi Menasseh Ben Israel also intended to cross the ocean. Moses Raphael de Aguilar and Jehosua Verlozing were governors of the Talmo. Abraham Mercado was one of the best physicians of Mauritstown. The famous physician Jacob de Andrade Verlozing was born in Pernambuco.

Conquest of Curaçao in 1634. (Far left)

The discovery of Curaçao as described by Ameriqo Vespucci, whose party supposedly encountered people of gigantic proportions.

The History of Curaçao

Curaçao, the largest island of the Dutch Antilles in the Caribbean Sea on the north of the mainland Venezuela, was discovered in 1499 by Alonso de Ojeda, who had Amerigo Vespucci on board with him. Before and some time after this discovery, the island was inhabited by hundreds of Indians belonging to the tribe of the Caiquetios, that also lived on the islands

It was also agreed that the West India Company would send ships to West Africa (Angola) for slaves and transport them to Curaçao, where they were to be received and sold off to local Spanish buyers by factors of the Genoese.

From 1662, till the end of the century, the great majority of slaves entering the Spanish Indies were shipped by the WIC (which held a monopoly in the Dutch slave trade) via Curaçao. From the moment that Spanish colonial officials conceded this 'legal' flow of traffic between Curaçao and the mainland – ostensibly to obtain slaves – there bloomed a regular, contraband trade in every sort of merchandise in demand among the Spanish

colonists in Maracaibo, Caracas, and the Spanish islands of Cuba and Santo Domingo. In this way, the Dutch effectively captured the Caribbean transit trade with the Spanish Indies and continued this well into the 18th century.

Influence and well-being

From the start, the Dutch Sephardi Jews played a central role in this lucrative traffic: they probably held more than a 20% share of the Dutch trade with Spain. More Sephardi Jews settled on Curaçao from the late 1650's and they dominated dealings with the Spanish American mainland through their contacts with the local Portuguese New Christian

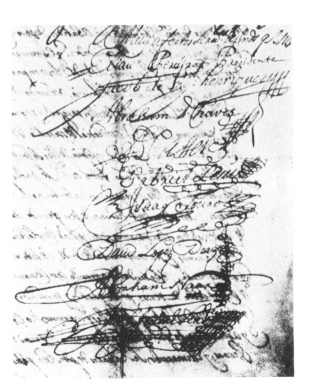

communities. By 1702, the Dutch Sephardi community numbered around 600 and accounted for 34,5% of the wealth on the island. Most of these Jews were agents, factors and brokers. The period of 1672-1702, corresponds to the period when the United Provinces of Holland were in open conflict with France but in alliance with Spain. There

Aruba and Bonaire. The island received its name from these Indians, or from a legend that says that the Indians fried a pastor (Cura-azado). More likely and scientific than this is the derivation from the Portuguese word Curacos, which means heart or cure. The Caiquetios belong to the Indian tribe of the Arawaks and were seafarers.

From 1499 to 1634, Curaçao was Spanish. In 1501, Alonso de Ojeda was appointed Governor. In 1513, nearly 2,000 Indians were evacuated by the Spaniards to Santo Domingo to work in the copper mines. In 1527, the Spaniard Juan de Ampués began the real colonization. Cattle and seeds were now shipped to Curaçao. Only a 150 Indians remained on the Island to look after the cattle and the agriculture. The Spaniards converted the population to Christianity. Of the 450 islanders whom the Dutch found there in 1634, about 250 had already been christened. During the Spanish period cattle-raising was the principal means of subsistence. The export of cattle skins was very important. Another means of subsistence was the trade in 'Red Slaves'. After 1527, Curaçao became a port of transit for red slaves hunted down on the coast and carried here to be shipped to Hispanolia (The present day Haïti/St. Domingo).

In 1634, the Dutch conquered Curaçao after defeating the Spaniards. At this time, the Netherlands and Spain were at war and the Dutch were looking for a maritime base in the heart of the Spanish colonies. The Dutch West India Company, acting as executive body of the Dutch Republic, mounted an expedition under Johan van Walbeeck and conquered the island. Until 1648 Curaçao was a Dutch naval base. Trade with South America soared after 1678, when Amsterdam became the center of the linen trade. The great Amsterdam commercial houses had their agents here and Curaçao became an emporium for European products.

A view of the so-called savanna of the Jews in Surinam.

Signatures of Jewish notables of Curaçao, 1721.

can be no question that the greatest Sephardi contribution to Dutch economic influence overseas, and well-being at home, came precisely in the period of Holland's decline, not during its rise. The period of the War of the Spanish Succession (1702-13) marked a new phase in that for the first time since 1648, Spain was ranged on the side of France against the Dutch. The Treaty of Utrecht of 1713, restored peace to Western Europe and again the normal links between the Dutch Republic and the Spanish islands were reconstructed. The books of the West India Company indicate that the Sephardi Jewry continued to dominate a large part of the commerce with the West Indies. Their Caribbean trade continued to flourish during the 1672-1702 phase despite the persistent efforts of the English and French to penetrate the transit business with the Spanish colonies and to drive the Dutch out of the traffic to Barbados and Martinique. Despite the Navigation Acts it is obvious that much of the commerce of both Islands was still handled by Amsterdam Jews in the 1670s. However, the efforts of the English and French crowns, including Louis XIV's expulsion of the Jews from the French Caribbean colonies in 1683 did eventually have the intended effect. This pressure in turn caused a major shift in the pattern of Dutch Sephardi activity in the Caribbean towards concentrating on the resources of the Dutch colonies themselves.

During the 19th century, people on Curaçao lived by trade and by the shipping connected with it. Agriculture and cattle raising were never very extensive. This situation underwent a radical change in 1915, when Shell established itself on Curaçao. The opening of the Panama Canal was of considerable importance to Curaçao in becoming an important fueling station. In 1918, the Shell refinery was put in operation. In 1952, 11,000 people were employed by Shell Curaçao. The importance of Shell for Curaçao has been enormous. A world-wide industry of this size on a small and quiet island had economic, cultural, religious, moral and political consequences. The population increased from 33,000 in 1915 to about 149,000 in 1973. With the exception of the Shell refinery at Pernis in the Netherlands, the refinery on Curaçao was the largest Shell refinery in the world. The Sephardi Jews played and still play an important role in the oil business. Besides on Curaçao, Sephardi Jews settled also in other Caribbean areas. These will be briefly discussed.

Surinam

In 1639, the first Marrano colony was established in Torarica by Jewish Marranos from Holland and Italy. In 1652, English Jews arrived in Surinam (at that time an English colony). In 1664, the Sephardi community of today was established. These Jews came from Brazil via Cayenne, where they were expelled by the French. They established a colony on the Surinam River, south of the capital Paramaribo. They called it the 'Jewish Savanne'. They grew sugar cane which was exported to Amsterdam. Though there were instances of Amsterdam Jews investing heavily in sugar plantations and mills in Surinam, even before the Dutch captured the colony from the English in 1667, it was during the years that the Republic was at war with both France and England (1672-1675) that Jewish involvement in Surinam assumed

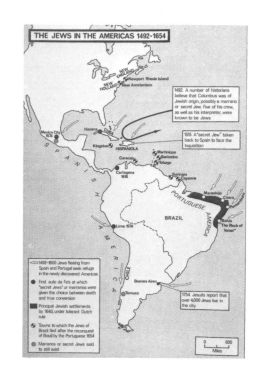

appreciable proportions. By 1694, the Surinam Dutch Sephardi community was the second largest in the Caribbean after that of Curaçao. They amounted to some 500, owning forty sugar plantations and some 9,000 slaves. Thus by the end of the century, Amsterdam Sephardi Jews had become the European corner of a trans-atlantic triangle linked to the Dutch Jewish colonies on Curaçao and in Surinam. By 1730, 115 of the 400 plantations in Surinam belonged to Sephardi Jews. The old cemetery in the 'Jewish Savanne' is still well preserved. On this quiet spot you still find the well-known names of Marranos: Cardozo, de Castro, Costa, de Matto, da Silva and de la Parra. In 1865, the Sephardic Synagogue in Paramaribo was consecrated; there is also a 'Jodenbreestraat' in Paramaribo.

St. Eustatius Netherlands Antilles

In 1722, there were four Jewish families (21 persons) living here. The total population amounted to 1,204 persons (including the slaves). In 1730, the Jewish congregation in Amsterdam asked for equal rights for the Jews living on St. Eustatius. In 1768, the majority of the Jews came from Amsterdam. Among them we find Joseph d'Ishac Mesquita de Lima, Joseph Bacra, Pretto Henriques, and Samuel d'Ishac Mendes Balboa. In 1739, the synagogue 'Honim Dalim' ('he who is merciful to the poor') was founded. In 1772, 'Honim Dalim' was connected with the sister organization at Curaçao, but also with the Shearith Israel Congregation in New York City.
On November the 16th, 1776, the commander of the island fired a salute from the Dutch fort 'Oranje', in honor of the flag of the rebellious English colonies from North America. The

Tombstone of Anjo David, son of Imanuel and Ieudith de Leao, 1760, on St. Eustatius in the Caribbean.
(Photo courtesy W. de Vrieze)

North Americans considered this as a recognition of their independence. It was the first time that this was done by a foreign power. The island was also occupied by the British Admiral Rodney. G. B., who robbed the Jews and took all their possessions. He then exiled them to various other Caribbean islands. The French occupied the island in November,

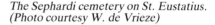

The Sephardi cemetery on St. Eustatius.
(Photo courtesy W. de Vrieze)

The Sephardi cemetery in Coro, Venezuela.

וַיִּקְרְבוּ יְמֵי דָוִד לָמוּת'

SEPULTURA

DO

ANJO DAVID FILHO DE

IMANUEL & IEUDITH DE

LEAO FALLECEO EM 4

TAMUZ A° 5520 QUE

CORRESPONDE 18 DE JUNIO

1760 DE IDADE DE 2 ANNOS

8 MEZES & 26 DIAS

Text on the tombstone of Anjo David (preceding page): 'Here Lyeth entered the body of David Haim Hezeciah, the son of Imannuel and Iedith de Leao, who departed this life the 4th of Tamuz 5520 which corresponds with the 18th of June, aged 2 years, 8 months and 26 days.

1790. At this time, 157 Jews still lived on the island. Around 1800, as the situation became worse, most of the Jews left.

St. Martin, Netherlands Antilles
In 1648 half of this island had a Dutch government, the other half belonged to the French. About 1755, descendants of Marranos arrived, such as Jacob Gomes and da Silva.

Aruba, Netherlands Antilles
In the middle of the 18th century, Jews of Marrano descent arrived. The first to appear were the Maduros from Curaçao.

Martinique, French Antilles
As early as 1654, Marranos had settled on this island.

Venezuela
Between 1642 and 1694, several groups of Marranos arrived in Caracas, the capital of Venezuela. There was also a Marrano colony in Coro and in Maracaibo.

The Cemetery on Curaçao

Curaçao has played an especially important role in the dispersion of Sephardi Jews in the Caribbean and, later, in North America. Nowhere else in the Caribbean had they gained such a sturdy base for their community as here. It will come as no surprise then, that on Curaçao some particularly interesting historic evidence of their stay can be found. The oldest synagogue in the Western Hemisphere, **Mikve Israel-Emanuel,** is on Curaçao, as well as the oldest Sephardi cemetery, the Beth Haim. To this day the family names of local bankers and businessmen betray their Portuguese heritage, such as Maduro, Capriles, Cardozo. But even more tellingly, the tombstones on the cemetery Beth Haim reveal the same unusual sculptured images as those found on Beth Haim at Ouderkerk a/d Amstel in the Netherlands. The rare visitor that enters the Sephardi cemetery on Curaçao nowadays will have to strain to see these truly remarkable decorations. The noxious gasses of the nearby refinery have all but wiped out the sculptures on the tombstones. In this context it is interesting to note the paradox inherent in this small tragedy. As it is strictly forbidden in Jewish law to move the buried, this prohibition was adhered to when Shell opened its refinery near the cemetery. After

all, there were influential Jewish agents that controlled all business in the port and thereby also the shipping of oil. It is obvious that the oil company did not want to upset their sentiments. Yet it is precisely this tolerant attitude that was to become the inevitable ruin of the tombstones of the old cemetery. Shell, while respecting the Jewish feelings, continued to expand its refinery by simply building around the cemetery.

Beth Haim on Curaçao was built around 1659 (the cemetery in Holland at Ouderkerk on the Amstel River in 1616). There are 2,569 tombstones (Matseiwot), 32 of which bear a

The oldest synagogue on the Western Hemisphere, Mikve Israel-Emanuel, on Curaçao.

The Synagogue Mikve Israel-Emanuel
This Synagogue is the oldest one of the Western Hemisphere, founded in 1732 (5492) on Erev Pesach, the birthday of Abraham Lincoln.
In 1651, the community of Mikve Israel was constituted. In 1674, the first Rabbi came over from the Netherlands, and in 1659 the first town synagogue was built. The present synagogue is the 4th house of worship that was built on the site then selected. It was constructed between 1730 and 1732 and modeled on the Synagogue of Amsterdam (the Temple of Solomo). The Hebrew inscription over the door is from Genesis 9:27: 'God shall enlarge Japheth and He shall dwell in the tents of Shem'.
The three stars over the word Japhet (the second word from the right) show that the letters in question should also be read as figures, i. e. as (5)490, the Jewish equivalent for 1730, the year when the first stone was laid. Another inscription on one of the doors reads: MA NORA HA-MAKOMHA-ZE ('How full of awe is this place') this 250-year old synagogue; this 330-year old outpost of Judaism. In 1982, the Synagogue existed 250 years. A commemoration book and stamps were published.

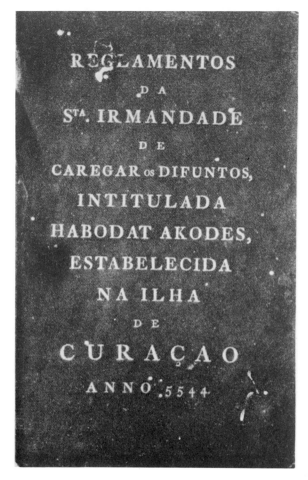

Dutch inscription, 40 in Hebrew, and 1,668 show an inscription in Portuguese, 361 in Spanish, 89 in English, 3 in French and 1 in Yiddish, while 260 bear no inscription at all.

The first Jew that came to Curaçao was Samuel Cohen (Coheno), an interpreter and specialist of Indian culture (he came from Brazil) who assisted Johan van Walbeeck in conquering Curaçao. Only in 1651, did the first group of Portuguese Jews headed by Joao (Jojada or Jan) de Yllan settle on Curaçao. They settled down on the plantation 'De Hoop' not far from the plantation Bleinheim, where later on they established the cemetery of Beth Haim. Who made the beautiful sculptures on the tombstones with the biblical scenes?

Interior of the Mikve Israel-Emanuel synagogue.

The official document establishing the cemetery Beth Haim on Curaçao.

In 1982, on the 250 year jubilee of the synagogue Mikve Israel-Emanuel, a commemorative stamp was issued.

73

The inscriptions on the graves are of historical importance: they offer information about the countries and towns that the Jews from Curaçao traded with. The age of the fathers, mothers, children and grandchildren are clearly indicated. There are many graves of the same family, so a genealogical family tree is easy to establish.

Beth Haim is also the resting place of Eliao Hiskiao Touro. He was an uncle of Ishac Touro, one of the Curaçao Jews who emigrated from Curaçao to North America with a group in 1693. The famous Touro Synagogue at Newport, Rhode Island, was named after the philanthropist Juda Touro, a son of Ishac. Another person buried at Beth Haim is Ribca Spinoza, half sister of the famous philosopher. She died in 1695 during a yellow fever epidemic.

A general view of the cemetery Beth Haim on Curaçao with the refinery in the background. (Photo courtesy Lex van Lith)

An old map showing the Beth Haim cemetery and surrounding plantations on Curaçao, about 1746.

The island of Curaçao did not contain any marble or limestone, and no trained sculptors. Through their family connections in Amsterdam, the local Jews obtained their blue tombstones, shipped by the West India Company. They imported the marble ones from Genua (Italy). The tombstones for the cemetery were chiseled in the Netherlands by Christian sculptors. They did not always comply with the rules of the Jewish law. Many biblical personages were depicted with uncovered heads.

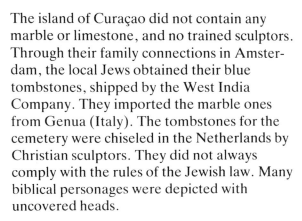
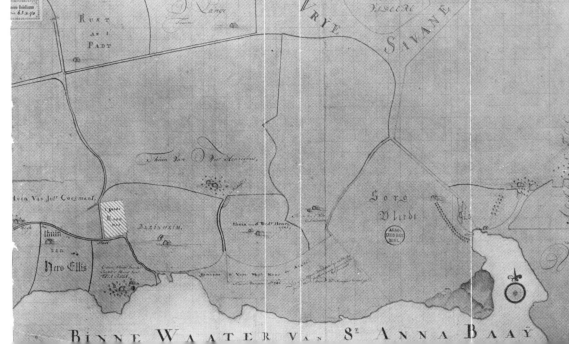

The oldest tombstone of potters clay on Beth Haim, Curaçao, belongs to Judith Nunes da Fonseca, 1668.

Beth Haim on Curaçao.

The inscriptions on the gravestones are of special interest in so far as that they tell us more about the areas and cities with which the Curaçao Jews traded. Also, they offer detailed genealogical information.

The outpour of noxious gases and fumes seriously damaged the tombstones, some to an irreversible degree.

Complete families have found their final resting place on Beth Haim.

A curious blend of Jewish law and Christian explicitness.

76

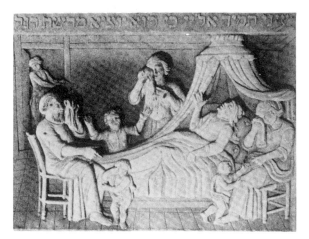

אם חמרים אלכים וכוי מוה יושא מרימה

Detail on the tombstone of Rachel Ieudah Cohen Henriques, 1767.

Detail on the tombstone of Miron de Benjamin Moreno Henriques.

Detail of the tombstone of Ishac Haim Senior, 1756.

Masonic symbols and two colums with the letters 'B' and 'I' representing a masonic temple distinguish the grave of David Haim Dovale, 1827. (Far left)

77

Arrival in North America

'In love of liberty and in defense of it,
Holland has been our example'
(Benjamin Franklin)

In 1654, the Portuguese conquered the relative small settlement that the Dutch had established on the Brazilian coast. Faced with the threat of persecution many Jews of Sephardic background fled. By means of Curaçao they eventually reached North America. At the time there existed a connection between Curaçao and the land that was to become the United States. The relation was based on the dual directorships of **Peter Stuyvesant**, a Dutchman, who governed both Curaçao and

New Netherlands (New Amsterdam, later to be named New York), and was one of the officials of the **first Dutch settlers.**
Yet the arrival of Sephardi Jews on the North American continent in 1654 was certainly not the first time a Jew set foot on this land. At least one Jew accompanied Christopher Columbus on his epic journey to the New World. This 'converso', Luis de Torres, traveled with Columbus on account of his knack for languages. He was one of the first ashore when the Admiral landed on the island of San Salvador in the Bahamas on November, 1492 (although the exact location is still disputed). Columbus' own supposedly marrano origin is still to this day debated by historians.
After the Sephardi Jews from Brazil and Curaçao settled in New Amsterdam – which was, incidentally, not readily approved by Stuyvesant – they set about to organize a form of community life much as they had done before in all the far away places that fate had brought them. They kept in touch with their kinsmen in Curaçao. The community there contributed in 1729 to the construction of the Shearith Israel Synagogue on Mill Street (New York). In 1764 again, they supported the debt incurred by the construction of the oldest

Peter Stuyvesant
Peter Stuyvesant, son of a protestant minister, was born in 1611 or 1612. As a young man Peter entered the University of Franeker in 1630. He did not finish his studies but instead joined the Dutch West India Company, serving it first in the Netherlands, later in Brazil (the Dutch colony Nassau), and from 1638 in Curaçao. In 1642, he became director of Curaçao, left the island for the St. Maarten expedition in 1644, lost his leg during a battle, and went to Europe for further treatment of his amputated leg. In 1646, Stuyvesant was appointed director-general of New Netherland and Curaçao; he arrived in New Netherland (currently New York) in 1647, and stayed till 1664, when he lost the colony to the English. He then left for the Netherlands, but returned to New York as a private citizen and died in 1672 at the age of 60 or 61. He was buried at St. Mark's in the Bowery, New York, where his tomb can still be seen. The tombstone, however, is not the original one, but relatively new. The original tombstone is to be found in the wall of the entrance hall. The dates on the stone are not correct.

Nieuw Nederland

Mohawk R.
Schenectady
Fort Orange Beverswijck
RENSELAERSWIJCK

Wiltwijck

Esopus Creek
Hudson
Connecticut

Manhattan Island
Haerlem
Pavonia
Nieuw Amsterdam
Governors Island
Staten Island
Long Island

Delaware

Nieuwer
Amstel
Fort Nassau

SWANENDAEL

five Dutch villages
Breukelen (Brooklyn)
Amersfoort (Flatlands)
Midwout (Flatbush)
Nieuw Utrecht
Boswijck (Bushwick)

five English villages
Middelburg (Newtown)
Gravesande (Gravesend)
Heemstede (Hempstead)
Vlissingen (Flushing)
Rustdorp (Jamaica)

synagogue currently existing in the U.S., the Touro Synagogue in Newport, Rhode Island. (Jews had begun settling in Newport – coming from the island of Barbados in the Caribbean – in 1677, nearly four decades after the Rhode Island colony had been established by Roger Williams as a haven for religious dissenters.) Besides New York, Newport and Philadelphia – which, by the way, had Jewish settlers well before the arrival of William Penn's Quakers – other major centers of Jewish life in the thirteen colonies were Savannah and Charleston.

The aforementioned synagogue in Newport has been designated as a national historic site in 1946. It was named after the philanthropist Judah Touro, a native of Newport, who left a generous bequest for the synagogue's upkeep. The building itself reveals a strikingly similar architecture to those on Curaçao and in Amsterdam. General George Washington, who by then was the first president of the newly United States of America, visited the synagogue in 1790, and proclaimed at the

t' Fort nieuw Amsterdam op de Manhatans

A view of Nieuw Amsterdam, displaying it as it was in 1630.

A map showing the location of Nieuw Amsterdam (New Amsterdam, later New York) and surrounding villages and forts.

First Dutch settlement in America

The earliest meeting between Holland and what now is the United States took place in 1609. In that year the VOC (The United East Indian Company) ordered Henry Hudson, an English captain engaged by the Company, to find an alternative route to Asia via the Polar seas. His ship 'De Halve Maen' (Half Moon) left from Texel in Holland. Hudson, however, failed to find the desired route; instead he sailed in another direction and arrived in North America. His enthusiastic report about possibilities for trading, especially in skins, led to the Dutch decision to concentrate on these regions. Several Dutch ships followed the route of the 'Halve Maen' during the next years looking for trade. On the basis of new information thirteen businessmen in Holland took heart and obtained a trading charter from the Netherlands States-General, the Dutch equivalent of the United States Congress. The charter gave the thirteen men exclusive trading privileges with the part of the East Coast that had already become known as 'New Netherland'. They chose an island on the Hudson River as their trading center, and erected a fort that was called Nassau. Fort Nassau was probably the second European settlement in the United States. (Jamestown in Virginia had been the first). It was the year 1614; six years later the Pilgrim Fathers landed in Massachusetts. The merchants of Fort Nassau carried on their fur trade for nine years. In 1621, Dutch pioneers bought the peninsula Manhattan for the amount of fl. 60,— (sixty Dutch guilders) from the Indians. In 1625, eleven years after Fort

time: 'May the children of the Stock of Abraham, who dwell in this land, continue to merit and enjoy the good will of the other inhabitants while everyone shall sit in safety under his own vine and fig tree, and there shall be none to make him afraid'.

From the beginning of the nineteenth century to the eve of the Civil War, the Jewish presence in the U.S. expanded from 10,000 to well over 100,000, as the total population grew from 5 million to more than 31 million.

Currently the number of Jewish Americans is estimated to be nearly six million or less than three percent of the overall population of 225 million.

Nassau, a new fort was put up on Manhattan Island. It was named Amsterdam, after the capital of the Netherlands, and the new town around it, New Amsterdam. During its last twenty years under Dutch rule, New Netherland changed from a trading post to a real colony (2,000 inhabitants). In due time, a community hall was erected; houses, taverns and commercial buildings followed suit. These were usually constructed along canals, much like the settlers had seen in their motherland, and more specifically, Amsterdam. In 1664, fifteen hundred people lived in the capital. In the same year they surrendered to English pressure. A peace was concluded which was judged to be rather favorable to Holland. England was to keep New Netherland; but Surinam in South America, which Holland had taken from the English, was to remain under Dutch flag. They then preferred a tropical country, complete with sugar plantations and slaves, to a settlement of white colonists.

Map of Nieuw Amsterdam.

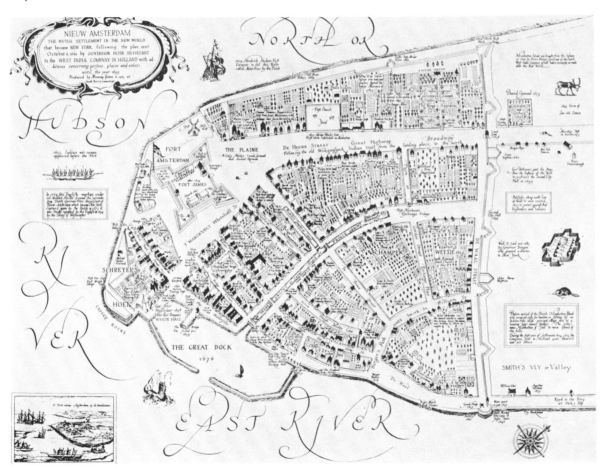

The ship 'Halve Maen' on which Captain Hudson reached the shore of New Foundland in 1609.

Date 5

Receptum November the 7th 1626

High and Mighty Gentlemen,

The ship 'the Coat of Arms of Amsterdam', arrived yesterday, sailing from 'New Netherland' (the east coast of Brazil), the 23th of September, coming out of the river Mauritius.
We can say that our people are living peacefully here and gave childbirth.

We bought **'The Island of Manhattan'** from the savages (Indians) for: **60 guilders**
Size of the land = 11000 acres.

We sowed all grain in the middle of May and reaped it in the middle of August. We now have samples of summer grain, such as wheat, rye, barley, buckwheat, canary seed, beans and flax.

The cargo list of the mentioned ship reads:

7246	beaver skins
178	half otter skins
675	otter skins
48	weasel skins
36	wild cat skins
33	mink skins
34	rat skins

Many beams of oak and walnut.

High and Mighty Gentlemen,
may we recommend you to the Almighty.

Amsterdam, the 5th of November
in the year 1626

I am your servant
signed by P. Schagen

Appendix

The Jewish calendar.
The difference between the Gregorian calendar and the Jewish one is about 3736 years. The Jewish calendar is a monthly calendar, which means that each new month begins with a New Moon. Because the monthly cycle takes 29½ days, the months have either 29 or 30 days. However at the same time, the movement of the sun is incorporated by a leap year, counts 13 months.

The date of the year changes on the first day of the month, 1 Tisjri (Rosh Hasana = New Year).
1 Tisjri is about Oktober 1
1 Nissan is about April 1
1 Tisjri 5710 = September 24, 1949.

Names of the months:
1 Tishri
2 Heshvan
3 Kislev
4 Tevet
5 Shevat
6 Adar (Adar II)
7 Nisan
8 Iyyar
9 Sivan
10 Tammuz
11 Av
12 Elul

The Jewish worldpopulation

	1930	1968	1985
Africa	503.500	196.200	153.000
Asia	682.700	2.544.200	3.515.800
Americas	4.759.850	6.952.450	6.492.700
Europe	955.775	4.019.000	3.278.800
Oceania	25.500	74.500	79.000

The most important dates in connection with the Jews in Curaçao, Netherlands-West-Indies.

1634 *Samuel Coheno* Arrives with the Dutch squadron with commander Van Walbeeck. He is the first Portuguese Jew in Curaçao.

1651 *Joaoa de Ilhao* He founded the first agricultural colony in Curaçao.

1652 The first Synagogue in Curaçao is founded, built of wood.

1654 Recife surrendered to the Portuguese. The Dutch are leaving Brazil. Many Jews settle in Curaçao. At that time the community 'Mikve Israel' probably came into being.

1659 Seventy Portuguese Jewish colonists arrive in Curaçao from Holland. They obtained a piece of land near Blenheim, there they founded the famous cemetery Beth Haim (house of the living), the oldest Portuguese-Jewish cemetery of the Western Hemisphere.

1674 *Josiao Pardo* The first Rabbi in Curaçao, arrives with his family from Holland. The first synagogue was founded in Punda.

1692 The foundation of the second synagogue.

1703 Founding of the third synagogue.

1713 *Jacques Cassard* He ransacked Curaçao. The Jews have to pay a quarter of a large ransom. At that time there were already well-to-do Jews.

1715 The Hebrew Charity Society was founded; they helped financially in many places, also by the building of Synagogues (in New York).

1732 The fourth synagogue is opened; this one is still in use.

1743 Consecration of the synagogue 'Neweh Sjalom'.

1750 Reconciliation between the governors of 'Neweh Sjalom' and 'Mikve Israel'.

1765 *Lopez da Fonseca* born in Curaçao, is chief Rabbi.

1856 *Aaron de Jacob Mendez Chumaceiro*, chief Rabbi, arrives from Amsterdam on the 19th of January with his family.

1858 The government of 'Mikve Israel' establishes a 'Midrash', a religious school.

1863 Disruption in the community 'Mikve Israel'. The origin of the Dutch Reformed Jewish society. In 1964, a merger took place, resulting in the United Congregation 'Mikve Israel-Emanuel'.

1867 The new Jewish cemetery on the Berg Altena is consecrated.

1869 *Aaron Mendez Chumaceiro* Chief Rabbi goes to Amsterdam on leave and sends in his resignation.

1927 Settlement of Asjkenaz Jews, especially from Eastern Europe.

1933 Foundation of the Society Union, representing the Asjkenaz.

1940 Publication of the monthly paper 'Mikve Israel'.

1941 Foundation of 'The Jewish Aid Society'.

1946 Establishment of 'The Jewish Foundation of Temporary Help'. Foundation of the Dutch Israelite community on Aruba.

1974 Solemn re-dedication of the Synagogue 'Mikve Israel' on Curaçao after its restauration.

1982 The Synagogue 'Mikve Israel Emanuel' on Curaçao, celebrates its 250 years jubilee.

Bibliography

Adelberg, Simon
De Marranen
Adler, Michael
The Emperor Julian and the Jews.
Agt, J. F. van
Synagogen in Amsterdam.
Ancona, J. d'
Delmidigo. Menasseh Ben Israel en Spinoza.
Anonymus
Die Päpstlichen Bullen über die Blutbeschuldigung.
Attema, Y
St. Eustatius, 1976.

Baer, Yitzak
A history of the Jews in Christian Spain.
Banning, J. A.
Amsterdam van A-Z, 1966.
Baron, Salo. W.
A Social and Religious History of the Jews.
Ben Chorin
Shalom 1980.
Ben Sasson
A history of the Jewish People.
Beth Haim
brochure 1973. Portugees-Israel. Begraafplaats te Ouderkerk aan de Amstel.

Bloemgarten, Drs. S. E.
De Amsterdamse Joden gedurende de eerste jaren van de Bataafse Republiek 1795-1798. In Studia Rosenthaliana, 1967.
Bloom, H. I.
The economic activities of the Jews of Amsterdam in the 17th and 18th centuries.
1st edition Williamport, 1937
2nd edition, 1969.
Blumenkranz, B.
Juifs et Chrétiens dans le Monde Occidental.
Bolten, Drs. J.
Tekeningen in de Albertina te Wenen en in de Hermitage te Leningrad.
Boon, R.
Ontmoeting met Israel. Het volk van de Torah.
Boxer, C. R.
Zeevarend Nederland en zijn wereldrijk 1600-1800.
De Nederlanders in Brazilië 1624-1654.
Browe, P.
Die Judenmission im Mittelalter und die Päpste.
Brugmans, Dr. H. K.
Geschiedenis der joden in Nederland, 1940 (with Dr. A. Frank).
Busch, Dr. H.
(with Dr. H. Hermans) Curaçao.

Bible
Old and New Testament.

Chumaceiro, A. M.
Zal het kiesrecht Curaçao tot het kannibalisme voeren? Curaçao 1895.
Crüsemann, Franck
Thora und christliche Ethik.

Dillen, Prof. Dr. J. G. van
Zeven eeuwen Amsterdam.
Dimont, Max
Jews. God and History.
Dubois, Marcel
Un regard chrétien sur l'Holocaust.
The Dutch Republic and the Hispano World 1606-1661.
Oxford; 982, 46-47.

Eban, Abba
Heritage.
Eckert, Willehad Paul
De haat tegen de Joden-Schuld der christenen?
Eeuwens
De West-Ind. Gids 1981, 12e jg 13e dl pg 360.
De eerste Jood op Curaçao. W.l. gids jg 193435, 16e jaargang, 17e dl pg 222.
Emanuel, Drs. I. S.
De Ned. Grafschriften op 'Beth Haim' of het oude Joodse Kerkhof op Curaçao;
Het oude Joodse Kerkhof op Curaçao in het maandblad LUX. Jan-Febr. 1944 no. 4.
History of the Jews of the Neth. Antilles 1 and 2.
Precious Stones of the Jews of Curaçao 1 en 2.
Emmanuel, I. S.
Seventeenth Century Brazilian.
Encyclopedie
van de Ned. Antillen.

Epkema, Dr. E.
Kroniek 1795-1812. Een Jodenkerkhof te Zaltbommel.
Evenhuis, R. B.
Ook dat was Amsterdam 1967.

Flavius, Josephus
The Jewish war.
Flannery, Edward
The Anguish of the Jews.
Fokkens, M.
'Beschryvinghe der Wydtvermaarde Koopstadt Amsterdam 1662'.
Fuks, Dr. L.
'De Zeven Provinciën in beroering'.
Hoofdstukken uit een Jiddische Kroniek 1740-1750.

Ganz, Mozes
Memorboek. Platenatlas van het Leven der Joden in Nederland van de Middeleeuwen tot 1940.
Geyl, Prof. Dr. P.
Geschiedenis van de Nederlandse stam 1961.
Gilbert, Martin
Jewish History.
Goodman, P.
The Synagogen and the Church.
Goslinga, Dr. C. C. H.
Emancipatie en emancipator.
Goudsmit, Ben
Citaat uit de Ned. vertaling van Shearith Israel, of lotgevallen der joden vanaf de verwoesting des tweeden tempels tot het jaar 1770.
Grayzel, Salomon Christian
Jewish relations in the first Millennium.

Grevelink-Bisschop, A. H.
Beschrijving van het eiland St. Eustatius, in bijdragen voor de kennis der Ned. en vreemde koloniën 1846.

Hamelberg, J. H. J.
De Nederlanders op de West-Indische eilanden.
dl 1. 1909, p. 3564. 101.102 117-136.
Dokumenten p 116 e.v. en 153 e.v.
Hart, W. ter
Curaçao in vogelvlucht.
Hartog, Dr. Joh.
De Ned. Antillen, Curaçao, Short History en Tula.
Hausmann, Dr. A.
De maaltijd van Belsarai in 'Oud Holland' 1967.
Hay, Malcolm
Thy Brothers Blood. N. Y., 1975.
Henriques de Castro, D.
Keure van Grafstenen op de Ned. Portugese Israëlitische begraafplaats te Ouderkerk 1883.
Hermans, W. F.
De laatste resten tropisch Nederland.
Heer, Friedrich
Gottes erste Liebe. 2000 Jahre Judentum und Christentum. 1950.
Hoetink, Dr.
De Curaçaose samenleving.
Huizinga, Prof. Dr. J.
Uitzichten. 1533-1584-1933.

Idinopolis, Thomas
Journal of American Academy of Religion.
Israel, Dr. J. I. Jacob
De handel in Amsterdam in the Golden Age.

Israel, J. I.
Spain and the Dutch Sephardim.
1609-1660.
SR 12 (1978) 5-6, 15-18.

Jaarboek van het genootschap Amstelodanum 33 (1936) 43-58.
Jessurun, Cardoza Is.
Ons Joods leven p. 106-122 in het 'Gedenkboek'; Oranje en de zes Caraïbische parelen 1948.
Jansen, Dr. Hans
Christelijke theologie na Auschwitz.
Jewish History Society
nummer 1, 2, 3, 4, 9 and 10.
Jewish Encyclopedia
New York & London Vol. iv 386-389.

Kamer, Henry
The Spanish Inquisition.
Kamer, Fr.
The Sephardies of Curaçao.
Katz, S.
The Jews in the Visigothic and Frankish Kingdoms of Spain and Gaul.
Keller, Werner
… En zij werden verstrooid onder alle volken.
De geschiedenis van het joodse volk na het bijbelse tijdvak.
Koen, E. M.
Notarial records in Amsterdam relating to the Portuguese Jews in that town up to 1639.
SR I (1967) 110-122 and 2 (1968) 111-115.

Laet, Joh. de
Jaerlyck Verhaal van de Verrichtingen der Geoctroyeerde West-Indische Companie in 13 boeken.

Lexikon
Des Judentums J. F. Oppenheimer New-York.
Lucas, Leopold
Zur Geschichte der Juden im IV Jahrhundert.

Maduro, J. M. L.
Gedenkboek Ned.-Curaçao 1634-1934. De
Portugese Joden in Curaçao p. 69-79.
Magall, Miriam
Kleine geschichte der Judischen Kunst.
Menasseh, Ben Israel
Catalogus van de tentoonstelling van geschre-
ven en of gedrukt door Menasseh Ben Israel.
Mennkman, W. K.
Aantekeningen op Hamelbergs werken.
Meyer, Dr. Jaap
Encyclopaedia Sefardica Neerlandica 1949,
Erfenis der Emancipatie. Het Ned. Jodendom
in de 1e helft van de 19e eeuw en Isles of the
Caribbean.
Miranda, Rodrigues da
Amsterdam en zijne bevolking in de 19e eeuw
1921.
Michener, James A.
Iberia.
Moehlama, C. H.
The Christian-Jewish Tragik.
Margolis, Max. L.
A History of the Jewish people.

Nachios, Dr. Bezabel
Spiegel van de joodse beschaving.
Neuman, Abraham A.
The Jews in Spain.

Oppenheim, Samuel
The early history of the Jews in New York.
Ozinga, Prof. M. D.
De monumenten van Curaçao 1654-1664.

Parkes, James
The Conflict of the Church and the Synagogue.
Polak, Prof. Dr. L.
'De betekenis van de joden voor de wijsbe-
geerte'.
Presser, J.
Ondergang. De vervolging van het Ned.
Jodendom 1940-1945. Delen I en II.
Poll, W. v.d.
Antillen en The Netherlands West Indies.
Publicatieblad
voor Curaçao, 1825. Nr. 95.18.26 nr. 103.

Quiros, Felipe Torroba B.
The Spanish Jews.

Rembrandt, Harmenszn van Rijn.
Beroemd hollands schilder 1606-1669.
Rokeah, David
The Jews in the Pagan-Christian Polemic from
its beginnings to the emperor Julian.
Rops, Daniel
Israel and the ancient World.
Roth, Cecil
History of the Marranos, A Short story of the
Jewish people and Personalities and events in
Jewish History.

Schepers, M. V. A.
A Documentary History of the Jews in the
United States, 1654-1875.
Schulte, Dr. C. M.
Nederlandse Expansie in Latijns Amerika.
Sharf, Andrew
Byzantine Jewry from Justinian to the fourth
crusade.
Silva Rosa, J. S. da
Geschiedenis der Portugese Joden te
Amsterdam vanaf 1593-1925.
Soetendorp, Abraham
Gesprekken en interviews.
Sousa Coutinho, Fransisco de
Correspondencia diplomatica de Fransisco de
Sousa Countinho durante a sua embaixada em
Hollanda 3 vols. Coimbra. 1920-55.
Starr, J.
The Jews in the Byzantine Empire.
Swetschinsky, D. M.
Kinship and Commerce.
The Foundation of Portuguese Jewish life in
seventeenth-century Holland.
'Studia Rosenthaliana (SR) 15' (1981). 55-57.

Tal, Uriel
Christians and Jews in Germany.
Trigt, Drs. F. van
Het epos van Israel.

Vaz Dias, A. M.
De deelname der Marranen in het oprichtings-
kapitaal der Oost-Indische Companie.
Vega, L. A.
Beth Haim at Ouderkerk
Veraart, Prof. Dr.
Joden van Nederland.

Vielmertti, Nicolaus
Die Juden in Osterreich während des
Mittelalters.

Waagenaar, Sam
De joden van Rome.
Wierink, P.
History of the Jews in Amerika.
Wizniter, A.
Jews in Colonial Brazil
New York 1960
46-7 120-138.
Wolff, P.
The 1391 Pogrom in Spain.

Zwarts, Dr. J.
Het echtpaar van het joodse bruidje van
Rembrandt; in 'Onze Kunst', 1926.

Alphabetical Index

(of the most important names)

Acknowledgements

Many friends, business acquaintances and other well wishers have helped me in writing this book.
To all I extend my warm thanks.
Then there are those who have been encouraging and others who have been especially helpful in the compiling of the innumerable facts, while yet others have assisted me in the composition of the text.
Of them I would like to name: Charles Gomes Casseres, Sjah Capriles, J. J. van Rijn of Nationale-Nederlanden Insurance Group, D. L. Rodrigues Lopes, J. R. Bienfait of the AMRO-bank, dr. J. I. Israel of the University College of London, the Provincial Archives of Middelburg, the State Archives of The Hague, L. Vega, the Portugese Israelic Seminar Ets Haim, Bart and Cheryl de Vries for editing this book.

Sincere apologies to anyone I may have forgotten.

A note on the type

The main text of this book was set in film in Times New Roman, a typeface designed by the British typographer Stanley Morison (1889-1967). The Times New Roman typeface was produced by Morison for the newspaper The Times. He created a typeface with an exaggeratedly large x-height in order to give the maximum amount of legibility, however small the size. The Times New Roman remains today one of the most widely used typefaces for publications requiring extended reading.

The text of the columns in the margins was set in Univers, a typeface designed by Adrian Frutiger in 1958. Univers, a member of the sans serif family, is one of the most popular typefaces today. Frutiger while designing it, took into account the effects obtained when using different printing processes. He produced a complete series of letters of different weights and outlines to cater to almost every purpose.

Composed, lithographed and printed by *Drukkerij Onkenhout B.V.*, Hilversum, The Netherlands.

Designed by *Arno Geels*, Den Haag, The Netherlands.

Of the first edition, 50 copies were numbered and authographed by the author. Of those, the copies numbered 1 till 30 are for the trade; the copies A till I are meant for the author; the copies I till X are destined for the printer.